WOMEN and
RUSSIA

Arkhangelsk

Petrozavodsk

Leningrad

Tallinn

Vilnius

Moscow

Sverdlovsk

Magnitogorsk

Nezhin

Donbas

Anapa

Alma-Ata

Samarkand

Erevan

Feminist Writings from the Soviet Union

Foreword by Robin Morgan

Translated by Rebecca Park and Catherine A. Fitzpatrick

SIBERIA

Kamchatka Peninsula

WOMEN and RUSSIA

Tatyana Mamonova, editor

with the assistance of Sarah Matilsky

BEACON PRESS   *BOSTON*

"The Other Side of the Coin" and "The Woman and Prison: A Conversation with Galina Zlatkina and Valeriya N." were originally published in *Freedom Appeals* (May–June 1980). "The Poster Woman" and "With the grandeur of Homer and the purity of Sappho . . ." were originally published in *Woman and Russia* (London: Sheba Feminist Press, September 1980).

Beacon Press books are published under the auspices of the Unitarian Universalist Association of Congregations in North America, 25 Beacon Street, Boston, Massachusetts 02108

Published simultaneously in Canada by Fitzhenry & Whiteside Limited, Toronto

Printed in the United States of America

(hardcover) 9 8 7 6 5 4 3 2 1
(paperback) 9 8 7 6 5 4 3 2 1

Library of Congress Cataloging in Publication Data

Main entry under title:

Women and Russia.

   1. Feminism—Soviet Union—Addresses, essays, lectures.
I. Mamonova, Tatyana, 1943–   . II. Park, Rebecca.
III. Fitzpatrick, Catherine A.
HQ1663.W63   1983   305.4′2′0947   82–73963
ISBN 0–8070–6708–3
ISBN 0–8070–6709–1 (pbk.)

Contents

v

Foreword

ROBIN MORGAN

In 1979, a group of extraordinarily brave women in the Soviet Union, knowing virtually nothing about the Women's Movement in the rest of the world, reinvented feminism. They wrote, typed, and circulated ten copies of the first feminist *samizdat* (underground publication), *Women and Russia*. After months of interrogation and intimidation by the KGB (Committee for State Security), four of the feminist "ringleaders" were finally sent into exile. Others still remain behind, writing under pseudonyms, trying to organize women.

These women are unlike any dissidents you've read or heard about before. They acted out of purely personal pain, rage, commitment, and vision—and without the prestige, contacts, or support available to such a major literary figure as Solzhenitsyn. They faced down opposition not only from Soviet authorities who accused them of treason and "counterrevolution," but also from many men of the dissident community itself, both in the U.S.S.R. and abroad, who accused them of frivolity and divisiveness. (It would appear that male supremacists everywhere have all read the same secret primer on How To Attack Women, especially those women merely demanding their minimal human rights.)

In August of 1980, I flew to Vienna for a week of intensive meetings with four of these women; the result was a set of interviews—the first in-depth articles about their personal and private lives—which I wrote for the cover story of *Ms.* magazine (November 1980). The days in Vienna were alive with embraces, shared laughter and tears, and an inordinate amount of strong tea. Tatyana Mamonova and I talked about everything

from our lives as women artists and activists, to our children
(both sons), to the militaristic orientation of our respective
male governments; when we came up for air, it was to take a
walk through the city, where we wound up putting antipor-
nography stickers on Vienna newsstands. After the story appeared in *Ms.*, there was a flood of mail from women in the
United States, reaching out to these sisters. That fall, *Ms.*
brought Tatyana for a visit to the United States, and she and I
toured the country, speaking together at almost twenty colleges
and universities. Everywhere we were met with warmth, open-
ness, and a surprise of recognition at the similarity of women's
condition in two such different nations. Indeed, as the articles
in this book make clear, Soviet and U.S. women share the same
basic situation of powerlessness. Our pain differs more in detail
than in kind, and our respective governments, while claiming
major ideological distinction from one another, share the same
patriarchal indifference to and suppression of their female
citizens. It is only by managing to accomplish that dangerous
conspiratorial revolutionary feminist activity—comparing notes
—that any women anywhere gain a measure of true sanity, perspective, and support.

For women in the United States, it has never been more important in history that we genuinely understand and commit
ourselves to the already existing and growing global Women's
Movement. As those of us who are deeply involved in that
movement know, this requires developing cross-cultural sensi-
tivities themselves invaluable in the world today; it requires
unlearning ethnocentricity and daring to look at ourselves and
our local movement as one vivid tile in a vast mosaic of
women's activism all across the globe; it requires the forging
of an entirely new kind of political and tactical sophistication
but at no sacrifice of an audacious idealism. The challenge is
great—and the rewards are greater: a revived sense of hope;

the miraculous recognition of shared experiences across language, racial, ethnic, cultural, and national boundaries; a renewed and empowering energy.

Especially today, in 1984, when the superpower Big Brothers of the United States and the Soviet Union both are rattling their nuclear sabers with a ferocity and a brinksmanship that could end all life on the planet before the year 2000, it is vital that women—who are, after all, more than half of the human species—speak to, listen to, and join with one another. There is no solution to humanity's agony so long as a minority of it holds (and abuses) power. *Feminism is the politics of the 21st century*—or there simply will be no 21st century on earth.

Women and Russia is the book in which Russian women speak for themselves. They speak to us from Leningrad and Moscow, from the Ukraine, the Urals and Central Asia, from Estonia, and Lithuania. They are not antisocialist but antitotalitarian. They expose the patriarchal structure of the Left as well as the Right, of their Politburo as well as their husbands, bosses, fathers. They express strength, rage, tenderness, irony. They are mothers and workers, artists, daughters and granddaughters, lesbians, wives, prisoners, activists, poets. These pages contain their stories, in each of their own incredibly courageous voices. In a very real way, these women are us. And we are them.

I can think of no more fitting way to end this Foreword than with the words with which, in Vienna, I greeted the first Soviet feminist exiles. In transliteration, they are, *Dobro pozhelozat vo vesmirny feminism, syostri:* Welcome to international feminism, my sisters.

December 1983
New York City

Introduction

The Feminist Movement in the Soviet Union

TATYANA MAMONOVA
Leningrad, Russia
Paris, France

The feminist movement has not long been in existence in the Soviet Union. It arose spontaneously in conjunction with the first appearance of *Woman and Russia: An Almanac to Women about Women,* of which I am the chief editor. The *Almanac* grew out of informal meetings in Leningrad in the fall of 1979 and is the first free feminist publication in the Soviet Union. Half of the *Almanac* is devoted to social questions, and the other half to the creative endeavors of women in general. Beginning with the first issue, *Woman and Russia* raised questions that had not been considered even by the dissidents: We addressed issues of interest to all women—women of every age, every segment in the population, every nationality—independent of persuasion. We provided a platform for all women—skilled and unskilled workers, housewives, students, and farmers. From the beginning, we have represented the mass women's movement and not an elite group. Furthermore, we advocate a positive program that in our view is in keeping with the nature of women. It is natural for women, who give life, to be opposed to war and violence—war of any sort, be it in Vietnam or Afghanistan, and violence against any being. We do not distinguish between guns and nuclear bombs, because all are weapons used for the death and destruction of people. Rather, we advocate an understanding of the value of life and of the value of women in sustaining and contributing to the quality of life through their full and equal participation in both the burdens and benefits of an egalitarian society.

It seems to me that in our time feminism is emerging as the strongest expression of humanitarianism. Yet in the beginning the *Almanac* did not receive the anticipated response (with the possible exception of Andrei Sakharov, whom we consider to be truly democratic) from the dissident men, who tend to be sexist. The dissident artists present themselves as nonconformists only in their art; in their attitude toward women, they are absolutely conformist. Like many other men in the Soviet Union, they have not grasped that the feminist movement is directed, not against men, but against the violation of the person in any manner for any purpose. I earnestly believe that the sexism of the nonconformist artists in The Second Culture[1] is the result of agents permeating the ranks of the movement.

The equality sought by feminists is not an arithmetic equality, for men and women are not identical. This was understood by August Bebel, a feminist and the author of *Women and Socialism*. It was also understood by Michel Montaigne, Charles Fourier, Friedrich Engels, Maxim Gorky, and others. These men understood that the position of women in a society defines that society and the quality of that society. Louis Aragon, Erich Remarque, Richard Aldington, and Lion Feuchtwanger also faced the questions surrounding women, and we had the opportunity to explore their ideas in the 1960s, during the short period of liberalization in the Soviet Union.

I count myself in the generation of 1968—the year of the occupation of Czechoslovakia and the rebellion in France. In that year we first started to think seriously about our way of

1. The Second Culture is a loose group of nonconformist writers, poets, and artists formed in the 1960s to protest the narrowness of the official artists and writers unions. Their informal literary evenings and artistic exhibits served as rallying points for those disenchanted with the system.

living and to doubt the fairness and prosperity of our society. But the illusions I carried before that year apparently remained with me, for when I was summoned in 1968 and questioned by the KGB about the case of a friend, I considered it possible to discuss freely with them a women's journal that I wanted to publish. They took notice of me then, for in 1979, when the first issue of the *Almanac* appeared, I was summoned first by the KGB even though there was no mention of the editor or publisher in the *Almanac*.

The KGB's reaction to the *Almanac* was stormy. They quickly understood that this opposition journal would not be narrow or elitist. Women constitute half the population of the Soviet Union and the *Almanac* discusses questions of concern to every woman: the conditions in maternity hospitals, abortion clinics, child care centers, and families. It talks about hard drinking and rape, single mothers and women's prisons—matters that affect every single woman. The KGB tried to dissuade me and to intimidate me. But new women kept coming to join the editorial staff, and with them they brought new strength. Then the KGB decided to take radical measures. On December 10, 1979—Human Rights Day and coincidentally my birthday—I received a present from the KGB. On this day of mine, as chief editor of the *Almanac,* I was given a severe warning: If there should be a second issue of *Woman and Russia,* I would be arrested.

We prepared to publish our second issue. Our modest undertaking had reached so far into world society that the ensuing publicity guaranteed us protection while we published the second issue of the *Almanac*—albeit under another name, *Rossianka* (Russian Woman). Western feminists visited us in Leningrad, and shortly thereafter the first and second issues of the *Almanac* were published in Paris. On the one hand this led to repression by the authorities—this time indirectly—and on the other it inspired us to broaden our sphere of activities. My home was watched by government agents. My husband was summoned to the enlistment office. We were both called in by the police, and threatened with charges of parasitism[2] and "private enterprise." In addition, the KGB persuaded our communal apartment neighbors to intercept our correspondence and prevent us from using the telephone. But our editorial staff continued to function, and if the first issue was only circulated in Russia and the neighboring republics (Estonia and the Ukraine), the second issue reached Kamchatka.[3] The third (which appeared in the fall of 1980) attracted the attention of women in the Caucasus, the Urals, and Central Asia.

I am often asked why I called the *Almanac Woman and Russia,* and why it is mentioned on the flyleaf that it was published in SPb (St. Petersburg). First, I chose Russia over the Soviet Union because there is an official publication for women called *Soviet Woman* and I did not want our journal to be confused with it. This choice seemed permissible to me because for most people there is no essential difference between the names America and the United States or between the names Russia and the Soviet Union. Second, I chose to refer to the city of publication as SPb for a specific reason. In our view, Lenin was a great revolutionary, but this does not mean that the city on the Neva established in Peter's time should have been renamed for him. I prefer the original name of the city, perhaps out of romantic sentiment.

The names chosen were not a matter of principle. Principles for us were the questions raised and discussed in the *Almanac.* We are not convinced our state is indeed socialist. For me per-

2. Parasitism, or having no officially approved work, is a charge commonly used against dissident artists and writers. In the Soviet Union, everyone has the right to paid work, but no one can refuse to work.
3. The Kamchatka peninsula on the easternmost end of Siberia is on the Bering Sea.

sonally, the ideals of the Revolution and of the pre-revolutionary movement remain bright and clear. In my opinion many wonderful women were an integral part of the Revolution: Sophia Perovskaya, Vera Figner, Inessa Armand, Vera Zasulich, Larisa Reissner. During these years Russia gave the world such great poets as Marina Tsvetaeva and Anna Akhmatova. During these early years feminism was understood and many were prepared to give their lives for their ideals. But Russia was too weakened from civil war, foreign intervention, and hunger to realize her people's dreams. On her bloodless body the parasite of Stalinism, of counterrevolution, grew.

During the period of the personality cult, all questions concerning women and the family were slighted or ignored completely. Russia's finest intellectual energies were destroyed and a generation gap arose. The neofeminist movement began in a virtual vacuum, for our women know almost nothing about the Russian feminist movement of the early 1900s.

I do not consider Khrushchev an ideal statesman, but it is impossible to deny that he assisted the people's cause in the 1960s. After the gloom and suffocation of Stalinism, Khrushchev opened the Soviet Union to light and fresh air. Several books about women's questions appeared, and films immortalized the work of such historical figures as the Socialist Revolutionary party leader Maria Spiridonova and the Bolshevik Alexandra Kollontai (Ambassador of the Soviet Union). In the 1960s Ekaterina Furtseva served in the government, and Valentina Tereshkova became a cosmonaut.[4]

I would like to say a few words about Tereshkova. Space flight was her greatest feat, but afterward the authorities used this achievement against women. Tereshkova was appointed

4. We consider the flight of the second Soviet cosmonaut, Svetlana Savitskaya, in 1982 as the official response to our feminist movement.

head of the Committee of Soviet Women, and for fifteen years I vainly sought membership on this committee. In the end I concluded that before a woman could sit on this committee, she first had to fly in space.

It is not difficult to write into the constitution Articles 35 and 53 guaranteeing the equality of women; it is considerably more difficult to realize this in practice. It is a faulty concept of emancipation that gave our women the right to do heavy dirty labor. In the Soviet Union, women do all the cleaning work; they work on construction and in building railroads; and they are trained for the most unskilled jobs. In Leningrad, 90 percent of the janitors are women. Before the Revolution this physical labor was generally reserved for men. And when women look to their homes, they see the same pattern: the work required to maintain the home is the women's responsibility. Patriarchal traditions are still followed in the majority of Soviet families. Women wait on the men and children, even though as a rule they work full-time outside the home.

When considering the position of women in the Soviet Union, many Westerners point to the number of women doctors, perhaps unaware that doctors are paid very little. Let us consider, for instance, a typical polyclinic. Clinic physicians, as a rule, are women, and they may see as many as thirty patients a day, which eliminates any creative approach to their work and the individuality of their patients. After work they must stand in line to shop for their families, carry the groceries home, and then prepare dinner. The heads of these polyclinics, as a rule, are men; they earn a considerably higher salary, have a significantly smaller workload and, therefore, can devote more time to writing dissertations or other materials. Of course, there are women who by a fantastic effort or a refusal to have families have made science their career. But these women are the exceptions, for it is not the state system that has made these achievements possible.

In addition, it is generally asserted here that women have a right to health care, but the conditions in maternity hospitals are of the lowest standard. My friends and I can attest to the level of care from personal experience. In these so-called maternity hospitals (actually closer to Calvary!) seven to ten women writhe on their beds and scream from pain. The attitude of the staff toward these women is one of contempt and annoyance. I must point out that the reasons behind the staff's attitude are obvious to those familiar with our maternity hospitals. The salaries are low, the staff are too few, and the work is brutal. This kind of environment is traumatic for women in childbirth, who require special care and attention. It may also be traumatic for the babies.

I gave birth in one of the major clinics in Leningrad. While I was there, I was not given permission to see my husband or to phone him. I was denied an anesthetic although the labor was protracted and hard. I was not able to take a shower for ten days—this is what I found in maternity hospitals. The experience was a nightmare.

In abortion clinics the conditions are worse. These clinics are simply production lines. They give abortions without anesthetics to several women simultaneously. In some abortion clinics women are tied to chairs. Strong women faint; mental and physical trauma is inevitable. Yet I know women who have had as many as fifteen abortions. We have no sex education. Contraceptives are in short supply, and those available are crude and ineffective.

I do not consider abortion bad—women must have the right to choose. The incidence of rape is increasing and women are often impregnated against their will. In such circumstances we as women look to the law to protect us. Formally, the law condemns rapists to five to seven years in prison, but fewer than 1 percent of Soviet women benefit from this law. In our society there reigns another law—a private law that forces women to bear the burden of shame for being raped. By these unwritten laws the woman herself is to blame for being beaten or raped or for having a husband who is a drunkard. We in Russia have heard of the Western antiabortion slogan, the "right to life." It seems to us that this slogan is more hypocritical than many of the Soviet slogans. For we think that the right to life belongs not only to the unborn but also to the woman who gives life. We do not call for the repeal of the constitution or of the judicial laws in the U.S.S.R. but rather ask that the constitution and these laws be observed. Most importantly, we call for social conditions that would make violence against women unacceptable in society.

Our Party elite does live under communism (provided by the state) and they worry very little about how the majority of the people live. Our gerontocratic government is locked in mortal combat, and evidently cannot cope with the problems facing it. At the helm is a rightist party although it calls itself Communist. The situation in the Soviet Union leaves much to be desired, but we believe that it is possible to democratize the country. We in our *Almanac* emphasize the need for a psychological revolution of consciousness, not a bloody coup.

The Soviet woman is educated in an atmosphere of falsehood. Beginning in childhood she is told that she is emancipated and that she is fully equal with men. Yet she is not taught about her highest function: to give birth to the next generation. Our girls receive the same education as our boys, but it is much harder to have a career. On the one hand they are called the "weak sex" and on the other they are given more responsibilities than men. Ideally, a woman is expected to have children, be an outstanding worker, take responsibility for the home, and, despite everything, still be beautiful. The situation of women is even more difficult in the countryside. They work the fields by hand; everything is on their shoulders. We cannot call this anything but a mockery of women.

Forces that should assist women in their struggle turn away from them. The Communist Party of the Soviet Union, for instance, has not given equal room to women. Women constitute half of the population of the Soviet Union but only 25 percent of the membership of the Party. The dissident movement has also shown little interest in issues affecting women and women's view of the problems in our society. Many émigré publications discriminate against women on all levels. Their coarse and indecent language abases the dignity of women, strips them of their identity, and reduces them to sexual objects. This language has not only penetrated the émigré press but become master of it.

The feminist movement in the Soviet Union is not a monolith; it comprises different philosophies and branches. There is a left wing, which is where I count myself; a nationalistic tendency is peculiar to the right wing, which encompasses Russian Orthodox women whom we consider elitist and affected. Orthodox women are now attempting to Christianize the feminist group Marya, which advances the ideals of the Virgin Mary. We consider these ideals inappropriate for contemporary women. Even if the concern is only with religion, this movement overlooks the people in the Soviet Union who are Muslim, Buddhist, Catholic, Jew, and pagan. The Marya group's efforts can only promote further divisions among women. By contrast, we are working through the *Almanac* to draw together as many women as possible. The third issue of *Woman and Russia* contains articles on the Central Asiatic, Caucasian, Baltic, and Kamchatkan women who are not Russian Orthodox; most of them are atheists. In the fourth issue we reach out to other groups of women through special articles about women in the socialist countries. We present interviews with women from Bulgaria, Hungary, Poland, Czechoslovakia, Yugoslavia, and Romania.

Women in the Soviet Union and the socialist countries are

completely isolated from the Western democratic women's movements. Many Soviet women call themselves feminists but know nothing about feminist principles. Our goal is to provide these women with information and the opportunity to express themselves—to give them the opportunity to be themselves. For example, it is no secret that there are lesbians in the Soviet Union as well as in the West. Soviet women with homosexual inclinations are forced to conceal their preferences and live in ghettos, for discovery may mean confinement in a mental institution. We think women should have the right to love whom they please. Life is little better for heterosexual women. The state allowance for single mothers in the Soviet Union is twenty rubles per month—enough to support a mother and child for one week, but by no means for a month.[5] Radio, television, and the press advertise the broadening network of child care centers, but in reality it is very difficult to enroll a child in a child care center. Both husband and wife must work, and even then there is a long waiting list. I, for instance, could not qualify to apply to either nurseries or child care centers because I did not have officially approved work but rather worked at home as a writer and painter.

The problems of women in socialist countries may not be unique to them, but many among us struggle in isolation to solve our problems, unaware that other women grappling with the same issues can come together to share their strengths, their efforts, their ideals, in their struggle to be fully valued as women. We consider it absolutely necessary, therefore, to create an International Feminist Union that would comprehend the position of women in the totalitarian countries and give them support. Through this union women could achieve optimal power and bring to an end the brutal treatment of

5. The stipend for single mothers was quadrupled, from five to twenty rubles, in 1982.

women now acepted as a norm. And through this union women of the socialist countries would be able to join with women in the West to share their views and experiences. Western women have their positive experiences and women of the socialist countries have theirs: the opportunity to compare experiences would be useful to us.

We took an important first step toward our goals in the Soviet Union. The *Almanac Woman and Russia* forced our authorities to move. The consequences were not solely negative. Yes, there were expulsions, arrests, and searches of women. But there was also a transformation of the official press. Within a year of the emergence of the feminist movement in the Soviet Union, many articles on the woman question appeared in the official press. Often the articles were purely rhetorical, but the questions were nevertheless raised—and that is the main point. People are now talking about these questions and are forced to think about them. Our state, which calls itself socialist, has found that it cannot completely ignore its moral responsibility to the people. The authorities were not able to eliminate the *Almanac* despite many efforts, and we continue to challenge the state to meet its responsibilities to the people and to Soviet women in particular. And if we frequently confront the Soviet authorities with their responsibility, change is inevitable. My dreams for change may seem naive to some, but I believe it impossible to betray the world—to choose an illusion veiling a deeper truth.

Working Women

Soviet economic needs and their ideology about women's equality have generally coincided. From its inception in 1917, the Soviet state has initiated educational and labor policies encouraging women to enter the paid labor force, in effect implementing a sustained affirmative action policy. The results are impressive. The U.S.S.R. has the highest female labor force participation rate of any modern industrial society. The percentages of women in such professions as medicine, law, and engineering far exceed comparable Western rates. Similarly, the percentages of women engaged in agriculture, construction, and metalworking remain high.

Despite this achievement, however, major problems remain. Women have achieved a level of economic independence, but they are still overconcentrated in low-paying jobs. Within the professions, the higher-paying, higher-status jobs still go mostly to men. Barriers to career advancement inherent in women's double burden of work and family responsibilities have not been adequately addressed. For example, part-time or flex-time work is not generally available, and newspaper articles discuss the difficulties for women in combining career and family.

These difficulties may increase if policy-makers worried about the declining Russian birth rate implement measures designed to encourage new mothers to take longer paid leaves. Similarly, worry about women's reproductive role seems to be behind more stringent protective labor laws, approved in 1978, which expanded the list of occupations prohibited to women (among them, work as carpenters, bus and truck drivers, and subway train engineers). Nevertheless, as the next article indicates, neither legislation nor custom bars women from much of the backbreaking, menial work of Soviet society.

3

Woman Worker

VALENTINA DOBROKHOTOVA
Petrozavodsk, Karelia

I work at the train station in the mail transport department. I am taking courses to become a railroad conductor. Working as a train conductor is one of the better ways to travel around the Soviet Union. Otherwise, travel is almost impossible since travel passes are expensive, "camping out" is hard, and hotel rooms are at a premium. It is also dangerous, especially for women, who risk being raped; rape is very widespread in our country. Young people, students, and just plain adventure-seekers often take jobs as conductors on trains that are traveling to faraway places. But most often it is middle-aged women who hold these jobs, for practical rather than romantic reasons. For me, too, it turned out not to be romantic after all.

Not long ago, we were assigned to the parcel division to help catch up with the goals of the plan. It was one of those times when they called on everyone to work. We worked twelve hours a day. Ten of those hours, and sometimes more, we spent unloading and transporting carts laden with packages. It was virtually the same job as a freight loader. We were only given thirty minutes to eat during both day and night shifts. Sometimes our team would not meet its quota in the time allotted to us, even when we worked harder than usual, and someone would have to stay and work a few extra hours.

What is surprising and disturbing is that only women work this unbelievably labor-intensive job. Among four teams working in the package division, there was only one man—the team leader. The rest of the men would rarely put in an appearance, and then only when they felt like working overtime. Women

5

were never asked if they wanted to work overtime: the extra hours were simply considered their duty.

A similar situation exists on our construction sites—a clear example of the exploitation of women. Even if the proletariat in our country is no longer an exploited class, women are now exploited twice as much. This abuse is not reflected in the laws, but it exists in reality. By law, women are not supposed to lift weights over twenty kilograms (forty-four pounds). But if the weight of the packages does not exceed this weight, it is assumed that a woman can lift this same weight over and over again, countless numbers of times. Here in our post office, the norm or quota is three hundred packages per person per day (during a holiday season the quota is as high as five hundred per day). Each package weighs from seven to ten kilograms. Thus, all together, a woman must lift more than two thousand kilograms (forty-four hundred pounds) in one shift and during "holidays" four to five tons. Thus, on the First of May (Labor Day) or the Seventh of November (the anniversary of the Soviet Union)—the days marking our great socialist revolution—a woman will break weight-lifting records. But she does not hear the applause that rewards the male weight lifter.

In addition to this, the woman worker must walk great distances, since the train station is very large. Assume that the mail cart is placed in the middle of the room and the packages are lifted and carried to various places. During an average day, each woman must carry packages a total of two to three kilometers, and five kilometers on "holidays." When you take into consideration the additional effort to pull the carts around, working conditions seem entirely oppressive. If each package weighs about ten kilograms, the worker must move from 350 to 1,000 kilograms. One woman pushes this load, straining herself to avoid bothering her busy coworkers. And women must struggle even more when the cart wheels are jammed. This is not unlike the work in the pre-revolutionary salt or coal mines. There is good reason for women here to worry about pain in the lower abdomen and to complain about the backbreaking work. I experienced the truth of these words myself.

Women even work the night shift for twelve hours in a row, just as on the day shift. It is as if the authorities have completely forgotten that the nature of a woman's body makes work in such conditions harmful and the effects of this labor sometimes irreversible. This is especially true if a woman is pregnant or menstruating or recovering from an abortion (which happens quite often because good contraception is unavailable here).

In the Soviet Union it is taken for granted that women will work on railroad beds, on road crews, on construction sites, and as janitors or cleaning ladies. Certainly men do not relish the prospect of sweeping out passenger cars, cleaning up after drunks, endlessly wiping tables, making up berths, and cleaning out toilets; as a result, conductors more often than not are women who have been instilled with the idea that this is "women's work." It should not be surprising that some women leave this "women's work" for prostitution, which flourishes in our train stations, preferring even that humiliating "profession" because it gives a woman at least some measure of freedom, some degree of choice.

Of course, prostitution is ruinous for women. I do not want to justify it: I would like to point out the reasons behind it. Prostitution is a form of escape, and yet the woman really goes nowhere. She runs away from domestic exploitation and ends up in industrial exploitation; she runs away from both the first and the second, and ends up being sexually exploited. Yet, ironically, prostitution has become a euphemism for women's freedom, a freedom that society condemns. In our country, women from any level of society who demonstrate even the least sexual independence are called prostitutes or worse.

This kind of society could hardly have been what people had in mind when they dreamed of a socialist society. Revolutionaries could hardly have meant this, for there were many great women among them. Sophia Perovskaya, Vera Figner, and Larisa Reissner (poet and commissar) gave up their lives for socialist ideals.

Today a woman has no outlet for complaints because women's sections[1] have been abolished as "unnecessary." It is becoming increasingly clear that the current equality means only giving women the right to perform heavy labor. In the past, heavy work was confined to the home, but in our day the woman, still not freed from the incredible burden of the family, strains herself even harder in the service of society. The situation described above is true not only in large cities but also in villages. On collective and state farms, women do the hardest and most exhausting work while the men are employed as administrators, agronomists, accountants, warehouse managers, or high-paid tractor and combine drivers. In other words, men do the work that is more interesting and more profitable, and does not damage their health.

Women have limited access to the technical fields; they are rarely accepted in schools of technology. In this area, the prevailing stereotype of women as people incapable of mastering mathematics and technology comes into play. It is as if administrators had never heard of the outstanding mathematician Sophia Kovalevskaya or the famous scientist Marie Curie, not to mention the thousands of other women who work effec-

1. This reference is to the Zhenotdel, or Woman's Section, established in 1919 by the Bolsheviks at the insistence of Alexandra Kollontai and others concerned about addressing the specific needs of women. It was abolished in 1930, as was the Jewish section.

tively in technological fields. Officially the state expresses concern for women's health, and statistics designed to prove the many efforts of the state are staggering—but in real life, something quite different staggers you. You sense that the functions of a woman's body have been completely forgotten—functions without which the life of society would simply come to a halt. True equality consists of giving women the necessary knowledge and opportunity to meet the same standards applied to men, and of making allowances for biological differences between the sexes. Equality is not simply giving women the right to shovel manure.

Translated by Catherine A. Fitzpatrick

Interview with a Career Woman

GALINA GRIGORYEVA
SVETLANA SONOVA
Leningrad, Russia

We met each other one Sunday at the Russian Orthodox Cathedral on the outskirts of town. Recently, young educated people have been gathering there on Sundays. I will answer the question how this came about at another time. For now I will only just say that once again it was a result of women's initiative. Let us turn now to the Career Woman, which is the name she and I agreed upon. I found I had something in common with her right away because I, too, have a university education and a background in the sciences. She, in turn, was very enthusiastic about the work I am currently involved in (I should more accurately call it a part of my life, albeit a secret one)—exploration of feminism, religious groups, and mystical searches. Ever since we met, the Career Woman and I have been meeting to talk every Sunday. When I asked her to give me an interview for "the feminist movement," she immediately and enthusiastically agreed, which perhaps says the most about her. Her answers to my questions poured out in an agitated monologue, so I use the term *interview* loosely.

Q. What are the most critical problems in your life?

A. Oh, there are a whole lot of them—where *don't* you find them? First of all, there are professional problems—my future scientific work. Then, there are great material difficulties—poverty, unsettledness. And then there are the problems that

just have to do with being a woman, the experiencing of yourself as a woman.

*Q. What kinds of problems do you have in your professional
work? Tell us about them.*

A. I graduated from college, went to graduate school, and
became what is called a qualified young specialist with good
prospects. I then became a fairly decent worker in my field.
All that took time—about ten years. I like my profession, my
work, the section I'm in. It seems to go without saying that
my work is important and necessary in industry. After I began
my own independent work, I had my first disappointment: It
didn't matter what I did or didn't do, I still got the same
response—no. To an intelligent person it's clear right from
the start what is wrong: the way the management is set up. It
is almost impossible to get something through that is new, progressive, or your own idea. The specific nature of scientific
work makes this worse. In order for scientists to see with their
own eyes the fruits of their labor, an invention must pass
through a number of stages. But so much time passes before
an idea can be put into practice that discoveries and innovations may no longer be practical by that time. You strain
every muscle to do something and end up beating the wind.
    Let me mention another characteristic of scientific work
here. Leadership has entirely disintegrated, and our work is
now ruled by the interests of the moment. The big bosses
cling to their positions through any means, and clearly have
no time for any progress in science. They only worry about
whether or not they're going to be dismissed. As professional
scholars in science they have stagnated—whatever talent they
once had has been used up. And we, the young specialists,
could give them a lot, but nobody appreciates that. A thick

layer of middle management is only concerned with preserving *privileges*. Their whole reason for existence is status symbols—a Volga automobile, a Ph.D., and so on.

Still another characteristic feature is the inflexibility of the system for job placement and incentive. The directors would probably be happy to triple my pay, and I would in turn produce more—really plow through the work—but that's not possible. It's hard to fire a poor employee, but it is also hard to encourage the talented specialist.

In order to achieve something, regardless of your talent or knowledge, you have to know how to climb the social ladder, and be willing to compromise your ethics. The majority of my colleagues are convinced this is necessary. I could do the same thing myself, but for personal reasons I can't be unethical or dishonest. After I finished graduate school, I worked for three years. I don't have all that much experience, but for the time being I am more or less satisfied with my position. But I sometimes wonder, What next?

There are incentives and encouragement; you can get bonuses, trips to the National Economic Achievements Exhibition in Moscow, raises in salary. But these incentives have nothing to do with your scientific achievements. They are tied to the way in which you conducted your work. There is no general belief in a simple human morality, not to mention scientific ethics. In the sciences we call such an approach "sawing the legs." And, sawing the legs has become widespread.

Q. What you have been saying is very interesting, but up until now you have been talking as "an average person" and not as a woman in the sciences. What can you tell us as a woman in the sciences?

A. A professional woman is treated scornfully in many cases. Despite high prestige as a scientist and publications, a woman senses a constant denigration. If I were a man, I would have been given higher-paying positions.

Q. How do you explain this?

A. It is the pattern of a slave psychology for a woman to place herself below a man. I believe women and men are partners in life and in science. But our emancipation leads to the woman becoming a man. It is not my "female" qualities that are respected at work. A sort of stereotype of the working person has been formed. In work relations, it is convenient for me to act like "one of the guys" and that suppresses my character as a woman.

I know, I sense, that by nature I am completely feminine, but I have stifled this femininity in myself. In the professional sphere I am not a woman but a "career person." That makes an impression on my psychology. If your husband or boyfriend treats you like a woman, that is acceptable, but at work that is bad—and I love to work. It is very likely that I have unconsciously imitated this stereotype—becoming "one of the guys"—and I feel that this has lessened me as a woman.

Q. What are the special characteristics of a woman who is a scientific worker?

A. I suppose it is easier for me to answer in general, as a career person. I think that if everything hasn't gone to pieces here yet, it is only thanks to women. Once in a great while you run across "very good" men who really move science forward. But the majority of them just drink vodka, and the average worker, on whom everything depends, is the woman. She is the chief executor. Thanks to her, a job moves forward.

Women with Ph.D.'s are not particularly liked and a relatively young woman, under forty or forty-five, with a degree is treated with mistrust and suspicion.[1] The possibility that she might have children is frightening to women like me, because that means she will not be able to work for a long period. Many women who have attained a certain level stop working and no longer grow in their field.

Women are also susceptible to status symbols. The question of prestige is a very important one at work. To be in a prestigious position means being married, having your master's degree in science, and having a good wardrobe—the chance to dress well. For example, it is prestigious to have good boots and a sheepskin or fur coat. Women especially want these things. But where does this get you? For me personally—in theory—I don't give a damn. I consider myself above all that. But in practice, I feel pressured by people's opinions which are formed on the basis of these things. For example, consider the problem of being able to dress well. Certainly I don't want to be a fashion plate; I would be happy just to dress nicely and be reasonably up to date. But the scarce goods—the fashionable or good-quality clothes and shoes—can usually only be obtained through corrupt, "under the table" methods at inflated prices, assuming you don't have the time or the inclination to run around town and stand in long lines. For example, I'm prepared to pay twenty rubles over and above the regular price for some nice, stylish boots if that's the only way to do it, but it's unpleasant for me.[2] I don't like having to deal with those people—the black marketeers—even though they hold respectable posts and aren't even called black marketeers. I

1. In the U.S.S.R., the doctoral degree is not usually conferred until a person has had considerable experience and published work in a field. To attain such a degree before the age of forty is considered a great achievement.
2. Stylish boots have cost at least 100 to 150 rubles during the last few years, that is, about a month's pay for a simple clerical worker or half the pay of the average professional.

don't like it; I feel like I'm "dirtying" myself by associating with them. It's also a sign of the demoralization of our society.

We often see foreigners walking the streets of our city. Without considering the details of their personal lives, just taking them at face value, you are envious. There is a shocking contrast between them and the majority of our women—even our educated women, even those who are not badly dressed. When you compare us with them, you are surprised at our lack of a culture of femininity: dressing nicely, carrying yourself well, simply being a woman. We just don't know how to do all that; our life ruins and represses this femininity in us.

And in yet another way, I have suffered as a woman, partly because I was wrapped up in my job, and partly for financial reasons, I couldn't have any children. I was sure that if I had a child, my life would turn into a domestic hell and, what would be hardest for me, I would lose my qualifications as a specialist. But you know, in the beginning I thought I was working for the good of society; this was something like a religious duty for me. Now I see that my efforts were pointless.

Q. Let's go on to another point you made earlier. You were talking about the material difficulties you had. Could you say something more about this aspect of your life?

A. You could call the situation tragic. The lack of money, never having enough, in spite of your relatively high pay—everything's so expensive, you can't buy anything. It's a very hard life. Before, life was a little simpler: if something was lacking, it was lacking everywhere. Now there are loopholes, channels, and those who know how to take advantage of them can live easier and better than the rest of us. Daily life just wears away our nerves, I think, more than in any other place in the world. People from other countries, especially from the capitalist nations, find it hard to understand us. Some foreign graduate students lived and worked with us. Even though they sympathized with us and even endured some of the difficulties of our lives themselves, basically they didn't understand and did not taste the full flavor of Soviet life. In any store, the salespeople may curse you, and they certainly do curse you. It's a chain reaction of meanness and irritability. Just to buy something you need a great deal of courage, because it is psychologically difficult to deal with the pervasive dissatisfaction with life that affects every person you deal with.

Women who have backups are to be envied—those with parents who are well off and still have their health; or grandparents who stay with the children and help out financially. A perfect example—but not typical—is my coworker. Including her bonus, she makes four hundred rubles a month, and her husband makes about six hundred. They're getting a car, but their parents are paying for it.

The most horrible and difficult thing for me is the nightmare of communal life.[3] It is a horror and a hell. In order to understand it, to imagine it and feel it, you have to live with it constantly. It's especially hard for an intelligent person to live among people who are not very developed and are entirely different—one likes loud music, another likes vodka. It is constant noise and chaos, racket and uproar.

There are five rooms and five families in our communal apartment. Each family has their own life style. There is, as usual, one neighbor who's an alcoholic. There is one family— a husband and wife and two small children—who live in a room twenty-two meters square. In order not to bother their neighbors or add to the frequent arguments, which are already bad enough, they do not let their children out of the room.

3. It is probably worth explaining here what a communal apartment is. In a large apartment of three to twenty rooms (on the average there are five or six rooms) several families live as neighbors, using a common corridor, kitchen, toilet, and bathroom (if there is one)—the same facilities for all neighbors. The situation has been ridiculed and criticized for some time—remember Mikhail Bulgakov's works—but for decades virtually nothing has changed.

Sometimes when I go by and look in through the open door, I see the father slowly and monotonously beating the children, punishing them repeatedly, and they don't even cry anymore; they just let out little yelps, from habit. This family has been on a waiting list for an apartment for ten years, and the prospects of their moving to a separate apartment in the next few years are not good. The most horrible thing here is the hopelessness.

I could give you a worse example, that of my friends who have children. Their communal apartment consists of three families. One neighbor doesn't work. He drinks all day, is completely dissipated, has VD, and during some of his binges, he excretes right on the floor in his room. There's practically nothing that can be done about it. The Children's Protection Commission is powerless to help in this situation. It isn't possible to exchange apartments (the so-called trades often mean higher rent). Who would move into a communal apartment? People in communal apartments are basically mean and rude all the time. They have no reason to be kind. Their interests are directed toward one thing: improving their material life. Their efforts have practically no results, but still take up all their energy. Living in contact with these people is very hard.

I could have moved to the provinces. Young specialists have tolerable conditions there—they are given separate apartments. But they risk losing the scientific milieu and becoming less qualified, because scientific life is at its best, at its highest standard, only in scientific centers in the large cities.

In general, the communal problems in our country are the grimmest nightmares. It's a constant stress, and you could never get along without taking *valeryanka* regularly.[4]

---

4. Valeryanka, derived from valerian root, is a commonly used sedative/tranquilizer in the Soviet Union. Our Valium also derives its name from valerian.

Q. What's the way out of this situation? More concretely, what do you personally try to do to compensate for this?

A. Only mysticism. I was drawn to this subject before, but that was just a little taste. Now I couldn't manage without it. For now, I won't dwell in detail on my explorations in this field, because there is still a lot ahead for me. For the time being, I will just formulate it this way: Where is the source of morality? It isn't in society. For us, Soviet intellectuals, the only way to draw spiritual strength is through religion.

Interviewer's Afterword

I have purposely omitted the specific scientific field of our Career Woman, her place of employment, and other details of her life. On the one hand, this is for reasons of secrecy, which are necessary for any activity in our country (even if it is harmless and naive) that does not fit into the narrow framework of the canon of "building socialism and communism." On the other hand, specific details were omitted to allow us to focus on the more typical aspects of her life. The Career Woman works in a certain field, perhaps the natural sciences, and I, too, in my day worked in the social sciences (that was a terrible time) and the picture is similar. What the Career Woman tells us of her life is true for many, many other Soviet women.

Translated by Catherine A. Fitzpatrick

The Poster Woman

IRINA TISHCHENKO
Nezhin, Ukraine

Her drawings are the embodiment of dynamics. Movement is the expression of her face. Her long fingers are restless. She is the most motor-mad person I know. Paralyzed when she was nineteen years old, she was too fond of her motor, her steed— a moped, bought with her first earnings. She pasted up posters. Those solitary and clear mornings when you are alone with your fantasies. The bright posters are like patches of rainbow in the mist. The little town lies in a valley. There are often mists in the valley. So there she was with her moped and some players from the visiting Chapiteau Circus. The players were on paper, the moped real. She loved it too much and once it abused her trust. Irredeemably. Forever. Or was the cause of it the mist? Only at that moment suddenly for the first time every-thing stood still. Everything that lived. Everything that was part of that incessant movement which delighted her, was es-sential to her ... Everything stopped. Her heart stopped. Clini-cal death. That is past. Past is the operation on her spine. All the fragments of bone were carefully pulled out of the spinal cord, but the spine refused to function. It had set. Frozen. Stiffened. Her life in a chair began. All the movement con-tained in her being was concentrated in her eyes. Even when those eyes looked steadily into yours, they seemed potentially to be preparing for movement. All the emotions that could be expressed, and would seem to be impossible to express, they expressed. The movement emanating from her pupils was, as before, infectious. It infected us, and we could walk.

And she drew posters:

21

Flying—the pigeons from under the magician's hand
Flying—the hands of the dance pianist
Flying—the eyelids of the spectators

following with bated breath the flight of the trapeze artist. Flying away the plane that was taking her to yet another town, where they again refused a repeat operation—too dangerous!

But she would not give up.
Flying on her poster, a new sun.

And in her chair, like the captain of a ship, she directed the world of her fantasies. Before she had not drawn, but movement was her essence, her foundation—it had to burst out into something.

And so was born the dynamic of lines, the play of color. And somewhere, pulled out of her skull, tightrope walkers continued to balance, wheels spun, performing dogs jumped, clowns tumbled on sawdust, fighting cocks flashed, jugglers tossed their props, tigers bared their teeth, trick riders galloped, motorcycles soared up in the ring of death, ridden by the celebrated mother and daughter . . .

Now I have become the poster woman in our little town. I visit the home of this remarkable person, who conceals an explosion within her, and I periodically despise myself for leading a life that's too quiet and measured. Maybe I should buy a moped.

Translated by the Women and Eastern Europe Group

Everyday Life

The stresses and strains of everyday life fall most heavily on the shoulders of women. Women do the bulk of the grocery shopping, a very time-consuming process. Supermarkets are still rare; shopping involves visits to several small stores (bakery, dairy, fruit and vegetable, meat). The Russians still adhere to a cumbersome method more appropriate to a time when most store clerks could not read or make change. Customers must stand in three lines, the first to order their purchase, the second to pay for it, and the third to receive it. This clearly discourages impulse shopping. On the streets, however, the shopper must be ready to seize any opportunity, for it is common to find a stall selling a hard-to-find item, such as toilet paper or oranges. Patience, or the willingness to stand two hours in a line, and preparedness (all Soviet women carry a net bag to hold unexpected purchases) are the key. Soviet men predominate on only one kind of shopping line—that for alcoholic beverages.

Despite official efforts to encourage a more equitable division of household chores, women do the majority of domestic work and child care. If a child is sick, the mother usually takes time off from her job to care for him or her. The absence of labor-saving devices or reliable services make household chores especially tedious. For example, Soviet washing machines are small and inefficient, dryers and laundromats are rare. The average Soviet woman resorts to the time-honored technique of boiling clothes on the stove to get them clean. In the countryside, the sight of groups of women doing their wash in the local pond is still not uncommon. Aside from the traditional domestic chores, rural women are also largely responsible for tending the family's private garden plot.

In the Northern Provinces

VERA GOLUBEVA
Arkhangelsk, Russia

According to the mass media, everything in the Soviet Union is wonderful. We have everything we need for complete happiness: a home, work, and apparently we are not starving to death. In general, if you listen to the radio or read the newspapers, we have complete prosperity in the Soviet Union.

But, if everything is in order, if everything is running smoothly, then people should be satisfied and happy. But if you look only at their faces, you find it hard to believe that they are very satisfied with their lives. People's expressions reveal worry, depression, or complete indifference. If you get to know them a little better, it becomes obvious that there is much they would like to change in both their personal and public lives. Women are particularly dissatisfied. Sometimes it is painful to look at them.

Tired after their workday, they hurry home to child care centers. Bowed with the weight of grocery bags, they drag their children behind them. In a terrible crush of people, they wedge themselves into overcrowded public buses elbowing people aside and pushing their way through to an empty seat, if there is one. At last, they reach home. Here, new cares await them: Dinner must be prepared and the husband and children must be fed. The laundry and housecleaning still awaits because, for a working woman, there is no other time for these chores. She cannot depend on her husband for anything.

The next morning, these women, with glum, blank expressions, take their children to school or child care centers and hurry to work. They perform their jobs mechanically, without inspiration, without enthusiasm. Consider the case of a working woman at the Arkhangelsk television station; you will see a disturbing picture.

If a woman television producer has a creative thought and experiments with an imaginative idea, the industrial-bureaucratic machine on which the progress of the country largely depends will crush that creative concept. Her enthusiasm will fade, and though on the threshold of inspiration, she will throw up her hands and close her eyes to avoid seeing her idea destroyed.

The monthly, quarterly, and yearly plan for meeting production quotas is necessary for any creative organization like television. Within these bounds the unscheduled day is considered one of the great benefits of working at such an organization. Yet there is no opportunity to use this unscheduled day creatively, for the bureaucratic machine moves into gear at precisely this point. The administration requires a compulsory forty-two-hour week, even if there is no actual output. It is not important *what* you have done during the day; it is important that you put in an appearance, serve your time to the minute, and record this in a special book which, if necessary, the administration can check to determine how many hours a week you still have to put in. Naturally, under such conditions, it is difficult to maintain normal creative ability. And the producer starts to torture herself, forcing ideas that should flow naturally on their own.

The economic aspect of life plays a major role in the general tenor of life as a whole. According to the newspapers, we have no unsolved economic problems. And there probably are no problems if you ignore the fact that in the city of Arkhangelsk, people simply have nothing to eat. The stores in the city lack even the most essential goods: There is no butter or meat or milk (milk for diabetics is available with special ration cards). There is no sausage or cheese or fish, although the city is a large, bustling port. The counters and windows are filled with dried soups and cheap canned goods. Apparently the authorities think this is enough for people to live on and work normally. On rare occasions, usually before the holidays, meat and fowl may appear; but when that occurs, you see what happens to people who have done without for a long time. With burning eyes, whole families struggle toward the golden place, and in two or three trips buy a kilogram or more of sausage, when only half a kilo is allowed per person. People are forced to buy products in large quantities, because such an opportunity does not come often. In the lines for meat, everyone is concentrating on one thought: "Just let there be enough!" Here and there you can hear people cursing; fights and scuffles break out. People become mean because they are struggling for a piece of meat they cannot buy even though they have enough money. It is particularly difficult here for women because they are the main hunters for food. This goes on at the very same time that radio and television emphatically report the rise in the standards of living of the Soviet people. It sounds so convincing that you might even envy them—whoever they may be. Every day for breakfast, lunch, and dinner, the Soviet people are served hefty portions of slogans which people have heard for so long that they are fed up to the teeth with them.

Why do the people not protest against this kind of life? Why do they not write articles for the paper or for journals? Why do they fail to talk about this on radio? The answers are clear to us: People know quite well that such articles will never be published in a single Soviet newspaper or journal. The Soviet "democratic" censor would not allow this. People are simply not allowed access to television and radio; letters sent to editors simply go into files.

Protests and demonstrations are not permitted here except for the demonstrations on the First of May when the people are compelled almost forcibly to march. There are few people who want to march in a parade and carry portraits of Politburo members and banners with slogans people are sick to death of. People are all the more resistant because they do not feel the slightest sense of solidarity with each other, much less with workers of the rest of the world.

Yet the question keeps arising: Why do people so passively and indifferently eke out a miserable existence? I think the answer could be this: The corrupt system of our supposedly socialist society has alienated the masses—the majority of the population. For this society fosters in its citizens an incapacity for united action and a life style that encourages the pursuit of self-interests.

Translated by Catherine A. Fitzpatrick

Why Soviet Women Want to Get Married

EKATERINA ALEXANDROVA
Leningrad, Russia

I happened to call an acquaintance of mine in West Germany and she told me that she was getting married in a few days. I started to congratulate her warmly, to wish her happiness, and to express my joy in general on the occasion of her marriage. To this she replied in an everyday, businesslike tone that she saw no cause for joy, on the whole, nothing special in the fact that she was getting married. She has known her husband-to-be for many years; they are living together, they have an excellent relationship, and they are both content with their lot in life. They decided to register their marriage officially because they are expecting a baby and it is easier to deal with the government bureaucracy if the child is listed as the product of a registered marriage. That way, she went on to add, all the papers will be processed normally and there will be no questions or misunderstandings. She could not resist making a few caustic remarks about the government bureaucracy and "this police state."

My initial reaction to her impending marriage had obviously surprised her and she asked how it was that I, an independent, educated person with a "male" profession, could attach any significance to such a worthless formality. To this I replied that I had expressed the usual reaction of a Soviet woman. In our country, official or civil marriage is considered a big step for a woman—perhaps the most important achievement in a woman's life, no matter how educated or independent she is and no matter how successful she has been in her profession. The stamp *married* in a passport confers innumerable social

benefits, and, perhaps more important, Soviet women need this
stamp for their own psychological sense of well-being, for their
self-affirmation. This need is created by thousands of little
things that are at times imperceptible but nevertheless create
a psychological atmosphere. Without that stamp, the Soviet
woman feels incomplete.

When she heard my explanation, this progressive German
woman was even more surprised and said, "Yes, this psychology
is well known in traditional, patriarchal societies, in which the
only place for women was alongside men as housewives and
raisers of children and the husbands were responsible for feeding the families. Women were respected according to the place
their husbands held in society. But surely in the Soviet Union
the situation is entirely different. There, women have the same
civil rights as men and the same opportunities for every type
of work. There, almost all women make their own living and
are materially independent of men." I did not bother this time
to set her straight and tell her that equality between Soviet
men and women is observed primarily on paper and that the
assertion that women have the same opportunities as men for
any type of work is pure nonsense. I had simply tired of speaking about the same thing so many times. (But I should have.
One must not tire of driving these truths into the heads of ever
greater numbers of people who were previously ignorant of
them.)

Yet, my acquaintance was partly right. There really is something to be surprised about and something hard to understand.
Here is a society that has proclaimed as its goal the extrication
of women from the narrow confines of the family and the in-
clusion of these women in all forms of public activity. And it
would appear that this society had achieved its goal—Soviet
women work at the most varied jobs, and many of them are
well educated, have a profession, and are financially independent of men. And yet, in this very society, among these very

women, a patriarchal social order and its psychology thrive.

I think that this woman would be even more surprised if she ever had to live the life of an ordinary Soviet, to observe Soviet life from within, instead of as a German tourist. Then she would see that Soviet women's aspiration to get married is not what it once was, in the "patriarchal society," but something new, something ugly and monstrous. One gets the impression that Soviet women are striving to get married and to hang on to their husbands much more intensely than "traditional women" can imagine, that they are capable of an absolutely furious level of activity in order to achieve this goal, and that they are willing to accept tremendous sacrifices and degradation of a sort "traditional women" have never dreamed of. This kind of thing is common in the U.S.S.R. But the most important thing is the psychology that makes it common—a psychology that is widespread and typical of the Soviet woman.

Something else that I imagine would have surprised my German acquaintance is the type of relationship that reigns in the average Soviet family. Dissatisfaction with another, mutual misunderstanding, difficult relations between the generations, and a deep-seated discontent with life all too frequently turn into open hostility and then into hatred. Strained relations in the family, constant arguments, and a lack of respect for one another that would surprise a "civilized" person turn family life Soviet-style into a living hell.

The general remarks I have just made are hardly capable of giving an outsider the true picture. Besides, some people who criticize modern Western life use similar words from time to time.

The reason for our present situation is that the Revolution destroyed the old social attitudes, the old morality, and the old customs. But the Revolution proved incapable of building anything good in their place. This is an especially large subject and I will not go into it here.

What is it that compels the Soviet woman to charge into the pit of marriage Soviet-style of her own free will? For it is precisely of her own free will that she marries, since she is financially independent, has a profession, and has at least some kind of work that gives her a definite social status regardless of the kind of personal life she leads. The Soviet woman does in fact have some degree of freedom and, in principle, can choose between various ways of arranging her private life. What makes her prefer, seemingly of her own free will, life in a nightmarish marriage that many married women openly hate and curse? What makes her pursue marriage with all the energy, persistence, vigor, and tenacity of a free person, "an architect of her fate," and not as a fatalist or a passive victim of circumstances? And after the experience of an unsuccessful marriage (or even several), why does she seek with paranoid persistance new attempts to create "a healthy Soviet family"?

The main cause for this phenomenon lies in the fact that formal civil marriage is supported officially in the U.S.S.R. to the highest degree. The desire for marriage is actively inculcated in society by the authorities.

This government policy was formulated sometime in the mid-1930s. Before that, in the 1920s, there had been a period of "freedom" and of experiments in marital relations. But since it was started, this official policy has continued with greater or lesser rigidity for almost fifty years. Throughout these years, the Soviet power has, as always, combined methods of "persuasion" with direct or indirect methods of "compulsion" (these methods have been stronger in some periods of Soviet history than in others).

This official policy has been implemented through three mechanisms: the judicial, by passing specific laws; the ideological, by the all-out, pervasive propaganda about "the healthy Soviet family" of socialist (and later, communist) morality and the condemnation of "amorality" and "dissipation"; and finally, the administrative, by effectively controlling and regulating the behavior of Soviet citizens.

Administrative control exists in various forms. To begin with, every Soviet lives with the certainty that the authorities are aware of all the crucial elements of his or her biography and that at any moment the particulars and the most minute details of his or her private life could become the object of the most intense scrutiny. In some cases a Soviet has a clear perception of being watched. From the outset Soviets know not to relate to their personal lives as if they were strictly their own business, something that, in principle, concerns no one but them. This awareness alone makes a strong impression on the behavior of a person (and incidentally, this awareness is painstakingly instilled in people "from the top").

On the subject of direct methods of administrative control, observable with the naked eye, so to speak, I will name two. One bears the outward appearance of "public control," but in fact, in its pure form, it represents a form of administrative coercion by the government (since all officially approved "public" activity in the U.S.S.R. is regulated from the top).

Most often the control of "the public" is exercised through examinations of bad or antisocial behavior at trade union or Komsomol (Young Communist League) meetings, for example. The person examined might be a drunkard, a person who skips out on work, or a person who has "fallen under the influence of bourgeois ideology"—the latter description is an extremely capacious formula, adaptable to many situations in life.

In recent years we have not heard about investigations of personal lives at meetings, although I heard from an acquaintance of mine about such a meeting that took place three years ago. It was a "court of honor" involving an officer who had taken it into his head to divorce his wife. But in earlier years —in the early 1950s, for example—similar "criticizing by the public" of people admitting to "amoral behavior" or "social corruption" (there were various formulas) were in great fashion. Another interesting example of these formulas: A man betrayed his wife and his behavior was discussed at a meeting, since he "demonstrated an uncomradely attitude toward a woman."

According to the reports of eyewitnesses, such meetings were extremely unpleasant procedures and everyone feared being the object of one. It is easy to imagine the shame and degradation you would feel with strangers rudely and familiarly digging into the details of your private life and holding them up for everyone to tear to pieces.

Another direct method of administrative control that has been around for a long time and is still effective and thorough is the following: In order to change jobs or positions, to get into an educational program, to go abroad, or to do a great many other things, a person must present a so-called reference card from his or her place of work or study. This is a piece of paper on which his or her superiors "characterize" the individual according to standard measures. Not the slightest change in a person's life can take place without this reference card.

A normal, positive reference card should contain the standard formula "politically mature, morally stable." This is a pure formality, a standard phrase that is written on a reference card automatically, as long as everything is going "as it should." But is it worthwhile for a person to move so far from the norm that her or his superiors would refuse to write this formula on the reference card? There is no easy answer. "Normal" life for this person would be finished. He or she would become a third-class citizen right then and there, the object of every kind of discrimination, a person whose opportunities have suddenly been drastically curtailed (and there are not many in the U.S.S.R. to begin with). As a result, Soviets are afflicted with a "precautionary fear" of crossing the boundaries (extremely vaguely defined) of what is permitted, "because you never know what might happen."

The administrative measures I have just described have long ceased to be widely employed for the control of a Soviet's "moral cast of mind in everyday life." They are now used for different purposes—first and foremost for guaranteeing the political reliability of citizens. Nowadays, if a person has been married and divorced five times, and has a dozen male and female lovers, all at the same time, this person will by no means be considered "morally unstable" because of this behavior. Furthermore, there is a feeling, an attitude, that if a person is interested in nothing but drinking, sex, and sports, then in the eyes of the authorities that person is "normal—one of ours." Such a range of interests is a kind of guarantee of social and political reliability, a kind of alibi. It is another matter if a person reads books or prays when not working. This is a sure sign that something is wrong, something is suspicious: "Who knows what that person may be thinking!"

Over a long period of time, the struggle for "control over morality" and the battle against "immorality" were conducted directly and widely, with the help of the measures I have described. Entire generations have grown up and been formed under the pressure of that control. Such, for example, was the generation of my parents. And this control played and continues to play an important role in defining the psychology and consciousness that induce Soviet women to get married.

Various "measures" like these were employed only when there was a question of "disorder" in official, registered marriages: for example, when spouses wanted to divorce—in the years when divorce was almost illegal—or in the case of adultery when the offended party complained, as we say, "up the chain of command." The offended party usually complained only when the marriage union was threatened (this was a serious ground for complaint), not when the offending party was discreet. As long as other aspects of a person's life did not threaten "the holy foundations of marriage," the government never interfered.

There are all kinds of grounds to believe that during World War II and immediately thereafter, the government quietly encouraged extramarital relations while it officially condemned them. After all, the country was in great need of the product of these extramarital relations—children.[1]

The government turned marriage into a kind of alibi for Soviets by instituting an official ideology that required a person to be "morally stable" at the same time it seemed to assert that the only possible way to be "moral" was to be married. No matter what a person did in his or her private life, as long as that person was listed as married and everything was in order in that respect officially, no statement of "unreliability" was issued. From the official point of view, the person was living "normally," "properly," "as one should," and according to the norms of "Soviet morality." But if a person was not listed as married, then that person's life was bad, abnormal, and either "immoral" or "incomplete" (like some kind of old maid). In Soviet "materialistic" society, there cannot be the respect for sexual abstinence that exists to one degree or another in societies in which religious traditions and morality play a role. Regardless of the circumstances, the government assumed that anyone not married was leading an incomplete, second-class life.

I wrote the last paragraph in the past tense, but everything in it is entirely applicable to the present. After all, no one has abrogated this official ideology and morality, and according to the government's ideology and morality, only a person whose marriage has been registered is living "as one ought," "as a complete person," and "morally." And this is something Soviets

1. I will consider this point in more detail later.

feel acutely in their contact with the Soviet bureaucratic machine, a contact that is intense, in truth daily, due to the colossal bureaucratization in all areas of Soviet life.

Soviets have to fill out a variety of forms and applications
in huge numbers for every conceivable reason, and are obliged
to carry them around from institution to institution. All these
applications, records, forms, and official papers are arranged in
such a way as to make you acutely aware that your status as
married is good or your status as unmarried is bad. (This is
only to be expected, since all this paperwork is a reflection of
official government principles.) Many women are keenly sensitive to the fact that writing *not married* in the appropriate
blank is shameful and degrading. And they strive to avoid this
all too frequent degradation at any price. (Incidentally, the
word *divorced* looks better than the words *not married* in the
eyes of Soviets, women included.)

To complete the picture, it is important to remember that
even now there are certain categories of people who risk incur-
ring colossal difficulties (examination at meetings, a ruined
reference card and, as a result, a ruined career) if they decide
to divorce or if one spouse files a complaint against the other.
These people are officers, diplomats, many of the people who
are allowed to travel and work abroad regularly.

After considering these characteristics, you begin to get an
idea of the kind of results you can expect from a system of administrative control over a "social morality" defined by official
Soviet standards. Many of these government people behave dis-
solutely in their private lives—at least when they are at home
and not abroad. But the family is everything to them—a screen,
an alibi, a social face, a guarantee of success. And they value
their official family positions greatly.

Let us turn now to a discussion of the laws that regulate
family and marital relations in the U.S.S.R.

As is well known, a series of laws governing such topics was passed in 1917–1918, immediately after the October Revolution. The main result of these laws was the secularization of marriage. Since then, as far as the government is concerned, the only valid marriage is a civil marriage, not a religious one. Therefore, when a Soviet woman speaks of marriage, she always means civil marriage; the word *marriage* has been used only in this meaning in this article.

In addition, the following policies were proclaimed: (1) freedom from restrictions that had formerly been imposed on marriage (for example, the religious denomination of the bride and groom); (2) freedom and ease of divorce; and (3) equality in every respect between "legitimate" and "illegitimate" children.

In the next round of legislation—the Laws of Marriage of 1926—the "freedom" of marriage was expanded even further, practically to the point that it was of no legal consequence whether the marriage was registered or not. In order for a marriage to be considered as legitimate, it was "sufficient that a man and women living together considered their liaison marriage and not debauchery." [2] Grounds for divorce were even broader and obtaining a divorce was made even easier. Divorce occurred without recourse to a court; it was not even necessary to be physically present. Divorce occurred in the absence of one of the spouses, by the declaration of the other. The equality of legitimate and illegitimate children was underscored. But with the new law of 1926, the period of "revolutionary experiments" in relations between the sexes came to an end.

The next legislative acts concerning the family and marriage —the Decree of 1936 and the Edict of 1944—were pervaded by an entirely different spirit. In the first place, in contrast with everything that had gone before, the new laws emphasized that

2. I. Kurganov, *Sem'ya v SSSR, 1917–1967* (Frankfurt/Main: Possev-Verlag, 1967), p. 89.

the only marriage considered valid in the eyes of the government was a registered marriage. The Edict of 1944 stated directly, "Only a registered marriage gives rise to the rights and duties of a husband and wife, as envisioned in the legal code of marriage, family, and child custody."

In the second place, the Decree of 1936 and the Edict of 1944 turned divorce into a difficult and expensive process. Furthermore, the Edict of 1944 pointedly began to separate "legitimate" children from "illegitimate" children. According to the law, the father of an illegitimate child had no responsibilities for his child, just as if he had no relationship to the child whatsoever. He was not obliged to help the mother support the child.

One measure that became highly controversial was the requirement by the Edict that a slash be drawn across the blank marked *father* on the birth certificate of an illegitimate child. This slash is the first thing that catches your eye when you pick up one of these documents. That requirement alone put both mother and child in a "special," extremely degrading position.

The 1936 Edict also banned abortions; these were permitted again in 1955 for medical reasons, and in 1968 without restrictions.

The other measures were eased only toward the middle of the 1960s when divorce was simplified and the slash on the birth certificate of an illegitimate child was no longer required.

Since the 1960s we have seen the monstrous statistics on divorce (every second marriage breaks up), which alone, without any additional explanations or comments, tell of the deep trouble running through Soviet families. (Only those who are allowed to divorce do so. Officers, for example, do not divorce. One of my friends is "married" to a sailor of the civil fleet who occasionally (rarely) goes abroad. They have long since stopped living together and have no personal contact, but they have not officially dissolved their marriage. If the husband divorces, he will not be allowed to go abroad anymore. The woman is content because she is listed as married, which eases her life considerably, especially in terms of her status at work. Her husband gives her lots of money for child support and brings her trinkets from abroad.)

The effect of the laws of 1936 was felt when there were relatively few men as a result of war, Stalin's repressions, and famine. (The same effect was felt when the Edict of 1944 was passed.) This situation by itself—the lack of men—under any circumstances would necessarily exert an influence on women's psychology and way of life. But at this time there was also an attitude that the only respectable position for a woman was as a married woman. This created an extremely difficult and degrading circumstance for women. After all, what was considered the only "normal" life was, for the majority of women, simply unattainable. And for that majority, existence remained second-class and incomplete.

Seeing the lot that fell to her unmarried friends, a married woman was happy, irrespective of the kind of marriage she had. For any unmarried woman, whether she was a widow whose husband had died during the war, repressions, or famine, or a woman who had never married, the state of marriage was a cherished dream, unattainable in practice and therefore all the more desirable. The most important thing, and sometimes the only thing, that women of that generation dreamed of for their daughters was marriage. This was the psychology that, in the direct sense of the word, we imbibed at our mother's breast—the belief in marriage "no matter what," the ambition to get married, the fear that a daughter would not get married. This powerful intense pressure—under whose influence we were raised—naturally had a tremendous influence on us, and our liberation from it came only after hard experience in life. (And have we really achieved this liberation?)

In the example of the laws of 1936 and 1944 (especially the

latter), it is obvious what sort of liberation the Revolution actually brought women. In reality, the Soviet system made women tremendously dependent on men, on the status of having a family, and on the patriarchal relationship and social structure, sometimes traditional but more often created anew by the Soviet system.

Especially striking is the clear bias against women and, in general, the extreme inhumanity of the Edict of 1944, which was passed in a time of war. The Edict of 1944 in no way made "the strengthening of morality" its goal. Not at all.

If it succeeded in making anything its goal, it was the strengthening of the morality of women, since the law transferred all responsibility for extramarital relations to them. The Edict of 1944 relieved men of all responsibility for extramarital relations and, most important, for illegitimate children. The law seemed to nudge the men, saying, "Go ahead! Seek your pleasure where you can find it and don't worry about a thing!"

At the same time the Soviet power was educating the people in the belief that extramarital relations were something dirty and shameful, it was training men to be cynical about their own numerous casual flings. Many women who got involved in such relations out of desperation became the objects of contempt for the very men they were in love with. (In fact, these women often hated themselves.)

On the question of illegitimate children, the Soviet government took and continues to take a position that puts women in a very difficult and contradictory position. Because of the huge loss of people during many periods in the history of the Soviet Union and the low birthrate, the government is extremely interested in achieving as large a number of children as possible and therefore tries in every possible way to stimulate the birthrate. Because of the country's poverty and colossal military expenditures, the government cannot allow anything more than a paltry allowance for children, paid maternity leave, and a few other measures that, in the aggregate, are clearly not enough to raise the birthrate significantly.

The authorities try to compensate for the insufficient material stimulation with moral stimulation, so to speak. The people are constantly being trained and educated through propaganda to believe, first, that life without children is not life, that only with children can a person live a complete life, and second, that it is a person's duty to society to have children. People who do not have children are egotists, living only for themselves and not for society, and they are, in general, antisocial elements.

The Soviet authorities extol procreation and maternity, and emphasize their respect for mothers in every way. It is possible that this education and the strong moral and psychological pressure lead many women to become single mothers. If there is no chance to get married and have a husband, they are at least able to become mothers.

Thus, on the one hand, any mother, including single mothers, officially enjoys great respect from Soviet society. On the other hand, a single mother, according to the criteria of that same society, is an individual of very dubious morals if not a downright loose woman. The complex, contradictory situation in which single mothers find themselves makes a "good" marriage seem attractive both to them and to those who observe their lives. In truth, it becomes "the ultimate dream."

As a rule, the life of a single mother is much more difficult materially than that of a married mother. On average, a man's salary is much higher than a woman's, which means that, in principle, a woman stands to gain materially by getting married. But I would not like to include the desire for a better material life among the basic reasons that induce women to get married, although there are women (and they are especially numerous of late) who strive to "marry well." For them material interests play an essential, if not the only, role. On the other hand, there are many women who are willing to make great sacrifices for the sake of getting married, and those sacrifices include material privations. It is enough to cite what has become a classic example—the number of women in the U.S.S.R. living with drunken husbands who drink up their wives' entire salaries and live on their allowances.

How did it happen that the Soviet power, having set as its goal the building of socialism and communism—in which, according to the classics of Marxism, the family is supposed to disappear, to "die out"—returned rather quickly to supporting the traditional family and over the course of time has maintained a rigid and active policy of strengthening this social institution?

The directive "to strengthen the family" that has come down to us from the 1930s does not, in theory, seem to abrogate the thesis that the family will "die out" under communism. The official attitude toward this question is expressed well by the words "In order to build communism and a communist family, we must strengthen the traditional family for the time being. Such is the dialectic!" (*Dialectic* is a good word. At will, it serves to explain both what is useful and how it is useful.) I do not remember when I first encountered those words in print, but they have etched themselves in my memory by virtue of their aphoristic style and typicalness. I have had many an occasion to encounter phrase-mongering of that sort.

How the Soviet power arrived at such a "dialectic" is, once again, a special subject that cannot be examined in a few words. I will just mention two points that I consider most important.

First, the basic feature characterizing a system of the Soviet type is the drive to control all aspects of human life. In this lies the ideological essence, the core of the system. Many have written and continue to write about this. I will not make any reference to anyone here. Second, I will simply say that all Soviets feel this atmosphere of force over them in their bones, although people perceive this to varying degrees. I can confirm this on the basis of my own observations over many years and my own experience.

The classics of Marxism discuss the nature of relations between the sexes in the new society: "This will be determined when the new generation grows up... When these people make their appearance, they will consign to hell everything that is prescribed to them today as their duty. They will know how to act and will develop accordingly their own social opinion about the acts of each person taken separately." [3]

But, in order for this to happen, people must be given free reign—without pressure "from the top"—to develop a new morality, a new type of personal relations that corresponds to life's new, altered conditions. Yet this is exactly what the Soviet system is incapable of doing. It is not that it does not want to—it simply cannot. By its very organization and structure, it is designed to maintain total control over every individual.

The question is, In what form is control over the personal life of an individual in this society possible?

Of course, an essential condition of such control is the inculcation in society of the idea that the construction of a new world requires people to be highly moral in their everyday lives and to devote all their strength, effort, and energy to the building of communism, of the new world—in other words, to devote everything to work, and nothing to their personal affairs. This immediately leads to limitations on and control of people's lives, or at the very least, of the lives of the people who pretend to the position of leaders. People who wish to transgress the rigid boundaries of permissible behavior in their per-

3. K. Marx and F. Engels, *Selected Works* (Moscow, 1952), vol. 2, p. 227.

sonal lives ought to be branded as "amoral," driven from the ranks of the leaders into the ranks of "the backward elements," and subject to the consequent discriminatory measures. One can speculate on and imagine the forms control in such a society would take. For example, a "community of wives" could be formed so that women could be paired off by bureaucrats.[4]

According to my information, there was no lack of risky or radical projects in the first years of Soviet power. And as far as I can judge, only the fear that they were too radical—"the masses have not yet matured to this level"—and that more than any other measures these might alienate people from Soviet power prevented these projects from being given a real chance. Furthermore, in the early years of Soviet power, when it was still truly capable of taking radical steps, it had too many other concerns.

Then came NEP (New Economic Policy); the "freedom" laws of 1926 coincided exactly with NEP. When the strong centralized power headed by Stalin later replaced "the rages of NEP" and the system acquired those characteristics by which we know it today, in many ways the system became rather conservative, concerned with little more than broadening and strengthening its own power.

To control the personal lives of citizens, the government identified a vehicle, and that vehicle was the family. Why invent something new when an organized form already exists and the framework of that form makes it possible to achieve total control over the behavior of the individual in his or her private life? After all, the family, along with its other functions, has always fulfilled the function of social control over the personal life of the individual. Only in the Soviet system did this function emerge as its first priority, the most important of several functions. Herein lies the peculiarity of the

4. Compare *The City of the Sun* by Tommazo Kampanelli.

Soviet family, its sharply pronounced tendency to concern itself with outward appearances, with "showiness," with the
observance of external forms, to an incomparably greater degree than the traditional family, or at least the modern family
in Western countries.

Moreover, the family also suits the Soviet system because it
allows the government to manipulate the individuals, to apply pressure in the necessary direction. After all, if a person
lives independently and does not value anything in life, then
he or she is less subject to social control and manipulation
than is a person who has something especially dear (no matter
what this happens to be, whether it be close friends and relatives, a favorite job, privileges, or something else). As a result,
the authorities try to find a niche for everyone, in order to keep
that person in their power. And the family, the children, become a trump card the authorities can play if necessary (and
they play it).

Another reason, not less important, that the Soviet power
took the course of strengthening the family instead of abolishing it is that the family in Soviet society continues to be the
economic cell of people's security in the traditional sense.

After the Revolution, the government intended to implement sweeping social measures aimed at abolishing the family
as an economic cell. This was one of the most significant
points in the planned program of reforms of society. It was
proposed that state-run kitchens be introduced, that there be
socialized child-rearing, and that in general women be freed
from their traditional domestic responsibilities. But everything turned out quite differently. After the Revolution, the
country's resources were thrown into maintaining and strengthening power—into militarization and industrialization—and
somehow there was "never enough" left over for social measures. For that reason the family remained the cell for social
security and for the support of children, the elderly, and

others. In order to ensure that the Soviet government would not be distracted by the needs of the common folk and be able to concentrate on the stated goals of industrialization, militarization, and consolidating its power, the family was necessary, and it was therefore necessary to strengthen the family rather than destroy it.

I will quote two passages from the book *Marriage and the Family*.[5] These two passages indicate the direction Soviet society was taking from the very beginning and elucidate what I have been saying. First, "The Soviet government was forced for a time to give up on the broad measures it had planned for public support of children, the unemployed, the disabled, and the elderly" and to transfer these functions to the family. Second, "With the existence of the family as a labor cell and especially as a cell of forced social support, it is natural that both the government, which for the time being has abandoned the idea of a common system of social support provided by the government, and individual people are interested in the incontrovertible registration of these cells."

But what does it mean that the family in the U.S.S.R. remains the economic unit in the traditional sense of these words? It means that the Soviet system preserves the traditional, patriarchal exploitation of women and that the family is the necessary means by which that exploitation can take place.

Thus, by attracting women to the work place and simultaneously preserving the traditional family, the system deliberately condemned women to dual exploitation, at home and at work. This is the "liberation" the Soviet power has brought women.

The more the government needs the family and needs to exploit women, the greater the significance of the propaganda

5. *Marriage and the Family* (Moscow, 1926), pp. 10, 21.

that fosters in women a desire to have children, that persistently and relentlessly inculcates in women the idea that only in a family can they find happiness, only by acquiring the stamp of *married* in their passports will they be complete as human beings. And the Soviet woman does strive to get married. Like a deceived little creature giving in to a tasty bit of bait that has lured the little animal into the trap, into captivity.

What I have written in this article does not by any means settle the question of why the Soviet woman wants to get married. There are other factors: old traditions, complex and multifaceted relationships between the traditional picture of the world and the specific picture of the Soviet's world; how a person has been raised; instincts; intuition. Actually, these are the reasons why women fall victim to Soviet propaganda, why a woman with a marriage Soviet-style dreams of a "real" marriage, about which she only has idealized and vague notions.

In this article I set for myself the modest task of attempting to show how the system incites in women the desire to get married. By destroying the old order, the Soviet power destroyed all the old patriarchal social attitudes. But in place of the old, destroyed patriarchy, the government introduced a new patriarchy that may be called a superpatriarchy. One of the striking manifestations of this superpatriarchy is the aspiration on the part of Soviet women to get married no matter what.

Translated by Rebecca Park

Zinochka Expands Her Circle of Bohemian Friends

Moscow, Russia

"Tantas Molis Erat Romanam Condere Gentam."
—*Virgil*[1]

Zinochka always read a book to get to sleep. She would read a little bit and fall asleep. And before reading, she would think over her plans for Saturday and Sunday.

In the middle of the night a child's cry awakened her, and shaken, she barely found her slippers, went out into the kitchen, and smoked a cigarette. Zina listened, carefully moved out into the hallway, and noticed with amazement the large number of strange coats hanging on the coat rack. Only a few coats seemed familiar. She listened for a bit. It was quiet. Then she returned to her room and was startled to find several people sleeping side by side in her room. Right before her, on the big chair, some clothing stirred and a baby cried. Zinochka's shoulders shook, and the cigarette fell from her mouth.

She quickly closed her door and bumped into a woman with a child, who politely asked her where the bathroom was. Zinochka showed her. The woman gave her the baby, she dutifully took him, and he started pulling her hair.

Zinochka and the baby collapsed onto the bed. But then she saw someone sleeping on the floor, and the sparkling eyes of her cat sitting on the edge of her bed frightened her even

1. "So massive a task it was to found the Roman race." *Aeneid*, Bk. 1, 1. 33.

more. Her heart froze, her head spun, her hands and feet were paralyzed. The cat stretched, jumped from the bed, rose up on its hind feet, opened its mouth wide, closed it again, and, darting past her feet, ran out. The baby pulled at her hair. Zinochka had no idea what to do with him, and saw no escape. She rushed to the kitchen, then to the bathroom, but the woman who asked about the toilet was not there. Once more another woman with another child asked directions to the toilet.

"I already have one," said Zinochka, frightened that she might get another child, but she pointed to the toilet.

A big puddle had accumulated from the bathroom, and Zinochka hugged the walls to hide from the woman, then dashed into the bedroom.

There the people had gotten up. Two older children stood on Zinochka's double bed with their shoes on, drawing red flags on her satin wallpaper. A third, with wet pants, shoved a chamber pot under the bed, vainly trying at the same time to fish out an already soaked part of the bed sheet from the pot.

Zinochka was speechless and could only stand staring at them and at the little girl with the red piping on her dress, who made a hill out of instant coffee on the parquet floor.

The telephone rang. Zinochka rushed to answer it, but a hefty man in dark glasses got there first. She stood and stared at him. He talked for a while, then called someone to the phone. The telephone rang many times. Zinochka never managed to pick up the receiver. Every time, someone dutifully picked up the phone, and each one greeted her. Children scampered by; the infant in her arms kept quiet and pulled her hair. And no one paid attention to her French silk nightshirt. Finally, the man in the dark glasses asked her, "Zinochka, why are you standing here all the time?" His concern touched Zinochka and she turned her eyes on the baby. "Put him down," advised the man, "nothing will happen to him."

Zinochka glanced around, found a place for him, and, to prevent his falling, set him on the floor. There, her cat, who was much bigger than the baby, touched its paws to his face, grabbed a corner of the baby's swaddling clothes with its teeth, and started to pull. Zinochka winced, and the bespectacled man (he was a professor and a poet called Lenya Dolgunetz, a pseudonym; no one knew his real name, but everyone knew that he wrote many books) tenderly took Zinochka by the shoulders and led her into the living room. There, around a gold table, on mid-nineteenth century gold chairs, people drank tea and coffee. Clothes hung on the backs of the chairs, and a beautiful woman in a feather jacket rested dainty toes clad in fashionable black slippers on an adjacent chair. Someone stood on an antique chair turned toward the window and opened the air vent. Thick smoke hung in the air.

"Sit down, Zinochka," invited Lenya Dolgunetz. "Yes, it's unusual to see such disorder at your place, but with so many people it's hard to keep clean," he said. "I'm very thirsty; we went to a wedding yesterday. He's a number one writer." At this point Zinochka remembered that Lenya Dolgunetz had visited her once, and his protégé, whom he called poetess number one, was with him.

He recited poetry, remembered Zinochka, and said that he had been the guest of a famous poet. (Zinochka forgot who it was.) And then he said that he drank a lot. And that at that poet's home there were only number ones and their protégés.

"And, as a specialist, I can say that this is a number one writer," said Lenya Dolgunetz.

He told about how they drank together, thought Zinochka.

"She is my student, a talented poetess," the poet continued.

There, too, there were only number ones, remembered Zinochka.

"Zinochka, please brew up some more coffee," commanded Lenya Dolgunetz.

In the kitchen Zinochka felt free, but suddenly she saw her cat. It sat on a stool next to the table and, it seemed to her, drank coffee.

I'll throw the cat out, she thought. It's big and can fend for itself.

When Zinochka brought the coffee, the room had undergone a change. The children were not in sight, the clothes no longer hung on the backs of chairs, and there were no longer as many people. Lenya Dolgunetz recounted something, but was particularly attentive to her and even stroked her back.

"Zinochka, why are you so unhappy? Never mind, you'll learn to cope. I would with pleasure have them at my place, but they don't want to go," he said to her.

"Yes, yes," said the woman in the feather jacket, "it's very comfortable for us here. We feel very good, and it's the center of town, no less. And we've already given everyone your telephone number."

"You'll get used to it, Zinochka," continued the professor. "Then it's easier to look at everything. Everything depends on a person's internal state. There are two elements of our psychic state that can be named conditionally: 'my bright sadness' and 'my dark sadness.' [2] In addition there are two twilight states: 'The Twilight State according to Fuchs' and 'The Twilight State according to Fügel.' Different combinations of psychic and twilight states define the psychological character of any given individual. The combinations can change depending on the circumstances, but the psychic state is in equilibrium when a person can find his or her characteristic combination under any circumstances. Thus, try to be yourself in any situation."

"Zinochka, some more coffee, please. Don't worry and don't pay attention to anything. Personal peace above all."

"And where are the children?" Zinochka asked timidly, wor-

2. The phrases "my bright sadness" and "my dark sadness" are taken from a poem by Pushkin well-known to Soviet readers.

rying that they might mess up something in her grandmother's study.

"Don't worry, they won't get lost," answered Dolgunetz. "I'm an expert on that question. I will teach you to be calm and even-tempered under any conditions. In life anything can happen. No one will explain these theories as clearly and as simply as I will. Yes, I spoke about balance. The Twilight State of Fügel is a feeling of soaring in a cloudless sky, a warm breeze pleasantly enveloping and rocking you, angels flying and singing all around you. The Twilight State of Fuchs can be described as a feeling of a swift fall into a pile of shit, from which you look up and see right in front of you someone's naked ass. Have I made myself clear, dear Zinochka?"

At that moment, the door to the hallway began to open slowly and let in a draft. Zinochka froze and her coffee cup dropped out of her hand. The cup fell slowly onto a saucer and then broke in half.

"Apartment number fifty, mine is forty-four. The apartment problem," spun around in Zinochka's head. "I paid my rent"—the phone rang loudly—"and for the telephone, too, or I paid for this month. Today's the thirteenth. Grandmother died. No, Grandmother didn't die. I died." Her head ached and buzzed. Zinochka did not understand at all what was happening. "I died, and this is a police check. Only, where are the police?"

Zinochka noticed the cat come in through the open door, holding something in its teeth that seemed alive.

"Where are the police?" she bellowed.

"I'm a policeman," Professor Lenya Dolgunetz answered laughingly. "What hurts? Where's the leak?"

"There's a leak in the bathroom," Zinochka shouted with glee and leaped up to run to the bathroom. But Lenya Dolgunetz laughed, grabbed her by the hand, put on dark glasses, lowered his head, and began to read poetry.

"I don't want poems," cried Zinochka. "I've both the Fuchs and Fügel states; different combinations look at red flags. I'll open a hotel on the shelves in Grandmother's room. And I'll throw out the cat. It's behind the table!"

"Zinochka, such a place you live in! A historic place. And who are you, anyway? One person in a three-room apartment. Is that why they don't divide up your apartment?" asked Lenya Dolgunetz. "Aidka, I found you an apartment! Divorce Simochka. He will marry Zinochka. And you will all live together. Three rooms are too many for Zinochka alone."

"I don't want to; I have a library," protested Zinochka.

"A library?" Lenya Dolgunetz mimicked sarcastically. "Yoga? All kinds of books? A three-room apartment? We know who you work for." [3]

"Who are you to talk," Zinochka retorted indignantly. "You! You write poetry, you have secrets, you go around using a pseudonym. Tell me your real name, psychiatrist!"

The door to the bedroom flew open, and Zinochka saw that on her bed, her beloved two-by-two bed, with its fancy inimitable German bed linen at twenty rubles per sheet, on her light blue artificial fur bedspread slept two strange men, fully clothed down to their socks.[4] With a naked woman between them. Her heart sank. But then Zinochka wondered why the woman was naked and the men clothed. She looked at the table. No one looked in that direction, except the professor whose eyes, even behind the dark glasses, shone brightly. Suddenly he jumped up, his mouth twisting and untwisting, and flung himself onto the bed. "Give the devil his due," he cried rapturously. "Give the devil his due, from the top of the nose to the tip of the toes." The woman kicked, and he cried, "Give the devil his due." Like a streak of black lightning, the cat

3. This is a reference to the KGB. KGB agents often have access to books and records forbidden to the general populace.
4. The bed measures two meters square.

flew past Zinochka and bit the professor's fat rear end. The professor twisted and turned, trying to free himself from the cat. And the naked woman—she it turned out was Aidka—held two children by the hands and screeched. The men woke up and looked around, completely baffled. And the cat scratched the professor's ass, bit it, and Zinochka heard the cat—she's sure of this—meow: "The combination of the Fuchs Twilight State and the psychological state of bright sadness gives one the sensation of a cat scratching your ass. Mee-ee-ow."

Lenya Dolgunetz dashed for the door, the cat jumped onto the bed, the two men, in their stocking feet, ran after Dolgunetz. The cat arched its back and opened its mouth. Then Zinochka saw that there was no one in the room, and the fur on the bed was all rumpled and torn.

The door opened and the voice of the professor cried, "The cat attacked me. Can you call the police?" "There's a leak in the bathroom," she answered him. "All the same, who died, Grandmother or me? If it was Grandmother, then that was three years ago, and if it was me—then, when? And this apartment, is it mine or Grandmother's?"

"Water flows, rivers flow, time flows, what else flows? I am in the Twilight State of Fügel, when you sit on your ass and you look at shit. All the same, Lenya explains things well."

Zinochka stepped into the hallway. No coats hung on the coat rack, but children's things and cigarette butts were strewn everywhere. There was smoke in the kitchen. Something was burning in the frying pan.

"It's night already. How quickly Sunday went by, and I didn't even notice." Zinochka began to count the vodka bottles on the table but lost count. "Today's the thirteenth, thirteen bottles—an unlucky day. Tomorrow work. Up early after cleaning all night."

The cat sat and cleaned itself. Zinochka went out. There were no coats. Cigarette butts were everywhere. "Today's the thirteenth, thirteen bottles." Zinochka tensed up with uncertainty; the cat rubbed against her legs and began to purr. It was very frightening. She left the kitchen, closed the door tightly, and also closed the door to the bedroom tightly. She lay down in bed, but did not go to sleep. First she read a little, because Zinochka always read a book to get to sleep.

Translated by Sarah Matilsky

Foremothers

On the surface, the bonds between generations seem much closer in Soviet society than in the U.S. In the large cities, the housing shortage and residency regulations combine to keep families under the same roof after a child's marriage and even divorce. The generation gap, immortalized in the nineteenth century by Turgenev's *Fathers and Sons,* and encouraged at times by the Soviet state (as witness the tale of Pavlik Morozov, the young martyr murdered for informing on his father), is generally treated negatively in the press. Alienated young rebels are condemned as antisocial individualists or spoiled children who don't understand true hardship.

Tensions between the generations do exist, but the Soviets, untouched by Freudian ideology and still mindful of the ravages of World War II, retain a special fondness and respect for their elders. This can be seen in small ways—special seats for the elderly and handicapped are provided on all public transport—and in larger ways—by the genuine affection between many mothers and daughters.

Grandmothers, or *bebushki,* have played a key role in the Soviet economy, compensating for the inadequacy of state-run child care. It is not unusual for a Soviet couple to leave their child in the care of a *babushka* while they pursue their careers. Grandmothers provide continuity with the past, and in Sinaneft's case, a glimpse at an older, freer cultural tradition. Reclaiming these traditions, discovering courageous and independent role models, and rekindling bonds with their foremothers are the goals of the writers in this section.

My Grandmother

Z. SINANEFT
Kamchatka Peninsula, Siberia

My Grandmother loved to travel. Her children (and there were more than ten of them) moved away and scattered in different directions, all going their separate ways. I will not even get into what became of her numerous grandchildren. Her children welcomed her into their homes as did many others. Grandmother led more than one generation into the forest in search of berries and on hunting and fishing expeditions. She could deliver babies and nurse the sick. I do not remember my grandfather, but Grandmother was something special. We were not actually together for very long, but I loved her more than anyone else. She taught me a great deal—how to sew and how to spin thread from nettles, saying as she instructed me, "Now we shall see just what kind of a master craftswoman you are." I remember how her head trembled (a bear had left its mark on her). I remember how we "hunted" for mice, how we gathered edible plants. She dug up tubers while I plucked the blossoms. The tuber from the lily is used in cooking.

I often heard that Grandmother had been a free spirit in spite of the number of children she had. She would leave her children with friends or relatives or, later, with the older children, and go off hunting. She hunted with her husbands (they say she was married more than once) and her grown children.

The hunting expeditions varied. In the winter she would hunt for furbearing animals; in the spring and fall, migratory birds, mountain rams, and bear. Most of the summer she spent fishing. When the various types of salmon began their swim

up river, she would barricade part of the river with a dam
made of willow stems. On one part of this dam there was a
"snout" or "muzzle" through which the fish could enter. Naturally she also left an opening so that some fish could go up-
stream to spawn. The fish that had been caught were taken
by cart to the village, and thus none of the villagers was left
without a supply of fish for the winter. When everyone had
enough dried, salted fish, the dam was removed. Fish were also
caught individually with a little hook on a long pole. No
native of Kamchatka can resist fresh fish soup served around a
campfire and aromatic tea made from water from the river!
Now it is forbidden to fish for salmon, but summer is not summer without at least one fishing trip. Like thieves we still
catch several fish and salt them for the winter. A native of
Kamchatka cannot live without fish.

And how many berries did Grandmother's hands gather!
After the first berry harvest, she would bake a pie. I do not remember the first time I personally gathered honeysuckle, but
at the age of five Grandmother stitched a small basket from
birch bark for me so that I could carry home what I had col-
lected. She treated the berry bushes carefully: She did not
pick them clean but left some for other berry lovers to enjoy.
As we returned home she would invariably break off a few
twigs from a birch tree for a switch. This she used to help
stimulate her "little bones" in the bathhouse. She healed both
people and animals, brought babies into the world and saved
their lives. I remember her assisting in a very difficult birth
by an older woman. The baby girl is a mother herself by now.

Once she and I saved a puppy that was drowning in a spring
flood. The family showed him to me several years later. They
named him Two Eyes, because he had white curved eyebrows
over his eyes.

As I was saying, Grandmother did not like to stay in one

place. She would often show up at my parents' home at the first crow.

In Kamchatka it snows a lot and two to three meters of snow will accumulate over the winter. Until the 1960s people traveled mainly by dog sled. Almost every family had a dog team. There were kennels that raised draft dogs. To make it easier on the dogs, people would travel from midnight to noon and from noon to midnight they would rest. That is why we used to say, "They spent the day at such and such hill or at such and such river." I remember well how people used to arrive and their stories about the journeys. Later I became familiar with these long journeys personally. You would lie on the sled (if you were a passenger) and look up at the sky and watch the changing constellations. You would arrive in a village while it was still dark and the first creatures to greet you would be dogs; the sound of many barking dogs would echo throughout the entire village. The people would wake up and, since the population was usually small, within minutes everyone would know whom the new arrivals had come to visit.

In the evenings Grandmother and I would forecast the weather for the following day. Through certain signals, known only to her, she was able to forecast a sunny day, wind, or rain. Our snow storms are especially heavy. A strong wind blows and it snows for several days, and after the storm all you can see are roofs and chimneys. In spite of this weather they continued to build low houses in Kamchatka.

In the fall we gathered sedge, which was used to make the insoles of a certain kind of footwear called *torbaza* (the boots are warm and do not hurt the foot). Sedge was also used to make mats used for window shades in the winter and for hotbeds in the spring. Grandmother knew how to sew *torbaza* with reindeer tendons twisted into threads. The Koryaks and the Evenis supplied the Itel'menis with reindeer tendons and milk.[1] Perhaps that's how she came to know the spirited Koryakian dance called Norgali.

I was thirteen years old when she died. I have not adopted all her ways but she left her mark on me. Perhaps it was through her influence that I became a traveler myself. I have traveled extensively throughout the country and I dream of traveling around the world. (My mother first laid eyes on a city at the age of fifty.) And when I wander the forest collecting mushrooms, berries, and herbs, I feel the harvest in my blood. When summer arrives, I stitch a basket from birch bark and go off to the woods. Those who remember her tell me, "You take after your grandmother."

Translated by Rebecca Park

1. The Koryaks, Itel'menis, and Evenis are all small tribes of Mongolian descent, living in eastern Siberia. The Evenis, numbering about 30,000, have their own national district. Raising reindeer, fishing, and trapping are the chief occupations of the tribespeople.

I'm from Armenia

TSOVINAR TSOVINYAN
Erevan, Armenia

My parents named me after the heroine of a national epic called *Samsa Tsrer*. Tsovinar was the progenitor of a great race. She was impregnated by water and gave birth to twins. The first handful of water produced the first child, but the second handful was less and thus the second child was born weaker. In the legend impregnation by water reflects, I think, the Armenian people's eternal dream of the sea. After all, though it is beyond our borders, the sea is not far from Armenia. Our famous Lake Sevan is not the sea, although there are many legends about it, too. This is natural, since our climate is hot and water is always in great demand. A second motif of impregnation by water instead of by a man is from the pagan world, when a woman's power was greater and sexual mores were different. A marriageable girl would bring an infant to an eligible bachelor as proof that she was capable of being a mother. In those times there was church prostitution, through which any young woman could acquire sexual experience before marriage. Perhaps that is why later, when the role of the father became more important, young families performed a ritual murder of the first-born. Because there was no certainty that the first-born had been fathered by the husband, it was assumed that the child was from an unclean source.

From the earliest times the husband proposed the first toast to the wife and the second to himself; this is still an aspect of patriarchy, since the husband proposes the toast and is considered the head of the family.

The death of the grandmother is honored by observing silence, and is always a great loss and misfortune for the family. The death of the grandfather was perceived as less of a tragedy. Armenians believe that woman is the keeper and maintainer of life and therefore she should live longer. It is as though the death of a wife before her husband leaves him without any function and renders him useless. It is cold and gloomy in a house without a woman.

Armenia has a very ancient history. Recently a classical Roman temple in Garni was fully restored; it belongs to the pre-Christian epoch of the second and third centuries. Our religion considers Christ a god but not God incarnate (Monophysites). It is basically an Orthodox religion but contains elements of Catholicism. Armenia has always attracted foreigners, with its natural resources, climate, and beauty. It was sometimes called Eden on earth and, according to one legend, the splendid gardens of Semiramis[1] were planted specifically in Armenia. A basilica surviving from the fifth and sixth centuries delights us to this day. There are traces of Syria's influence followed by that of Byzantium (seventh and eighth centuries). The Mongolian invasions of the thirteenth through the fifteenth centuries destroyed Armenia and Armenian civilization declined.

In general, Armenians are a long-suffering people. In April we observe an unofficial memorial day for the victims of the Armenian pogrom of 1915. The persecution of Armenians, and even efforts at extermination, increased during World War I. As a result, a comparatively insignificant part of the Armenian population remained. The fueling of national disagreement weakened Armenia still further. The slaughter of 1915 was perceived by people as a deep outrage and it has re-

---

1. Semiramis (c. 800 B.C.) was a legendary Assyrian ruler, famed for her military prowess and courage. She built such great cities as Babylon, and ordered the construction of large monuments. After her death, she was identified with the goddess Ishtar and her doves.

mained a wound that will not heal. We carry the memory of
Greater Armenia in our blood, an Armenia that thrived on
the glory of the people. In 1915 most of the male population
had already been conscripted into the Turkish army and the
pogrom was directed essentially against women and children.
In 1970 we organized a torchlight procession in memory of
the Armenian victims. The participants were mainly students,
including many young women. Young Armenian women are
freedom loving and many of them strive to achieve an education. They study in the institutions of higher education not
only in Armenia but also in Moscow and Leningrad.

I have not encountered many dissidents as such in Armenia,
but the echoes of the democratic and human rights movements have reached us. I have freethinking friends from artistic or intellectual circles in Erevan and Leningrad. In Moscow,
for example, I know the artist Artyunyan.

But I wish to return to the torchlight procession through
Erevan on a spring night in 1970. At that time the government
was officially celebrating the centenary of Lenin's birth. We
took to the streets two days later. Everything began calmly
and solemnly, and then the police began to follow us. I remember that many of the police were wearing shiny new medals
and badges on their uniforms, awards celebrating the first
hundred years since the birth of Lenin. The young people
began to get nervous. Some shouted slogans like "Up with the
Armenian nation" or "Up with Greater Armenia." But this
was not serious and it was not very intelligent. It was even
rather pathetic, because frequently those who were shouting
did not have even the most elementary grasp of the Armenian
language, yet they were taking it upon themselves to defend it.
Our procession quickly disintegrated and we tried to think of
what to do with the torches.

The Armenian people have been split up. Many Armenians
are living in Turkey (there is even a concept of a Turkish

Armenia). There are some Armenian settlements in the United States and some Armenian families scattered through Europe. This dispersion of Armenians prevents unity, although we have managed to preserve traditions and handicrafts and we have our own literature and theater. We are resurrecting the songs of the *ashugs*[2] (Sayat-Nova, Shirin, and others) and the songs of the singer-storytellers. Folklore and epic poetry constitute a large part of our culture. Theater portraying themes of everyday life arose only in the nineteenth century. The famous Armenian actress Siranush appeared in French melodramas and later in classical plays of world significance. The theater in which she performed represented the mood of the liberal bourgeoisie and noticeably helped raise the level of awareness among Armenians. Many experiments now underway are aimed at combining ancient and national stage arts; one is a silent stage art that contains penetrating psychological analyses appropriate for the modern world.

Women have great emotional depth and strive to express themselves artistically and creatively. Not long ago in the Caucasus a film entitled *Several Interviews on Personal Subjects* was released. The production staff included both Georgians and Armenians, and the film was dedicated to the lives of women. Sophia Chiaureli, the brilliant Georgian actress, played the leading role; her performance as the heroine was penetrating and warm. The heroine is a modern woman thirty years old, a reporter with her personal joys and sorrows, her home, her children, her unfaithful husband, and her fatigue. Chiaureli's portrayal of the reporter as she relates to other women, trying to help them and to ease their difficult lives is lucid. The film confronts the uniquely Eastern variant of a woman's fate. It also raises one of the most topical issues: the

2. Folk poets and singers from the Caucasus.

woman who has chosen to remain single yet bear a child. The heroine declares with a touch of pride that nowadays a husband is nothing but a hindrance, a creature of jealousy, reproaches, limitations, and no help at all.

Translated by Rebecca Park

Forty Maidens

O. KURBANGAEVA
Alma-Ata, Kazakhstan

In Central Asia in the territory of Kara-Kalpakya stands an ancient fortress bearing the name Forty Maidens or *Kryk-kyz-kala*. What is most surprising is that the title refers, not to a harem, but to "the land of women" (in old Kara-kalpak *forty* means "multitude"). The land belonged not to women recluses but to women defenders, protectors of the people. This fortress of the Middle Ages is associated with the name of the maiden-warrior (folk heroine) Aiparchi, Turkestan's Joan of Arc. Her sword felled a foreign khan who had encroached on her country. The khan was a clever, perfidious warrior, but Aiparchi had truth, justice, and the people of Turkestan on her side and her steed trampled the enemy's camp. Wandering minstrels composed a *destan*[1] about the noble avenger and her female friends. In the poem the heroine bears the name Gulain and the legend has come down to us through the ages to the present day under the title *Forty Maidens*. This *destan* can be called a protest against the forces of evil raging in the Middle Ages. Women knew the later terrors of Auschwitz during the Middle Ages when bonfires were set ablaze to burn "disobedient women" in village squares throughout Europe. Each village erected several bonfires, and contemporaries compared these with pine-wood forests. Researchers have estimated that about ten million women were tortured or killed by the Inquisition. In some small towns there were almost no mothers left.

1. Eastern nonrhyming epic poetry.

Moslem women suffered just as much. The laws of Islam did not defend women against the arbitrary rule of their husbands. They were denied their rights as mothers and the right to divorce. To this day the yashmak remains a symbol of the slavery of Moslem women in the Middle Ages and later. Women who dare to abandon their veils and seek an education commonly face savage mockery in Islamic countries. With Koran in hand, fanatics torture women. On December 15, 1930, Tursuna Jamilya Jumaeva, one of the first Uzbeki women to become a teacher, was brutally murdered by a group of religious fanatics. They murdered her when she was returning home in the evening after visiting some schoolgirls who had not shown up for their lessons that day. The murderers attacked her suddenly, tortured her at length, and then strangled her. And Tursuna was not the only woman to die that way. It is well known that even in our day, many backward men in Central Asia consider it shameful to be seen with their wives at a theater, club, or movie house, to walk side by side with them in the streets, or to have them seated at the same table with guests. There are still cases of polygamy, the rape of young women, and the exchange of a bride for a price. Fathers often impede their daughters' studies, husbands prevent their wives from working and, in general, men relate to women as master to servant. There are even instances of self-immolation by desperate women. To this day many women still wear the ritual covering, especially women in villages.

In contrast, it is especially uplifting to read the Kara-kalpak epic *Forty Maidens*, in which the spirit of Eastern women is praised. Legend has it that the people of Kara-kalpak (ancient Muitenis) trace their origin to a woman named Ak-Sholpan (White Venus), who was the daughter of a czar by one account, or of a slave by another. Her name was the battle cry of the Muitenis. The poem *Kryk-kyz-kala* describes how the beautiful Gulaim received part of an island as a gift from her father.

The area was called Miueli, which means "fruitbearing" or
"fruitful." A fortress was built for Gulaim on the land and
around it a moat was dug and walls were erected. The gates to
the fortress were made of steel and cast iron. The land in
Miueli began to resemble a large orchard. After gathering together women friends of her own age, Gulaim settled with
them in Miueli, far from any other towns or settlements. There
she trained them to be strong and courageous heroines and
skillful warriors.

> From her earliest years Gulaim was
> Intractable and bold.
> The day came when Gulaim
> Summoned forty maidens unto her
> And taught them to answer all
> Questions without hesitation,
> Vowing not to let their beautiful
> Hair down about their shoulders,
> To become real *dzhigits!* [2]

Islam, which forces young girls to cover their faces with a
veil (often starting at the age of twelve), and the Koran, which
contains the man's prayer thanking Allah for not having created him a woman, nevertheless have their contradictions. The
Koran says, "The daughter is dearer to Allah than the son,"
and "Don't strike a woman with so much as a flower." But
legends handed down to us attest to the greatness of the Eastern woman: Gulaim proves this better than anything else.

> Having grown fond of the noise and the daring
> Of the masculine game down to the depths of her
>   intrepid soul,

2. Caucasian horsemen.

> Gulaim organized a *toy*[3] with *kozlodraniye*[4] and
> fighting. She led her maiden friends onto a wide
> Green meadow and joined the battle games.
> The fast steeds were ardent
> And the maidens carried swords.

The image of a courageous woman from a place where for
centuries violence against women reigned cannot but delight
with its national strength and inner beauty.

But life in the fortress is by no means idyllic. In the next
stanza a courier representing envious suitors whom Gulaim
has spurned brings bad tidings.

> At precisely that moment
> Gulaim ordered the steeds to be brought out.
> At that late hour forty maids rushed to her,
> Having put on their shirts of mail.
> She hands them lances.

The maidens meet the courier. Gulaim has been slandered!
And then:

> The forty maids of Miueli
> Brought forty switches
> And bound his hands
> With a strong rawhide strap;
> The multitude then
> Caused him torment,
> Put him back on his horse
> Facing backward . . .

As he was leaving Gulaim said to him,

3. A Turkic festival.
4. Contests involving the roping and tying of goats, something along the
lines of a rodeo.

And so you have crossed my threshold
And have distracted me from my affairs.
You have brought me a stupid message,
You have demeaned our maiden honor.
Let he who may so desire babble nonsense.
Shame to the babblers and not to me.
It is not up to me to shut someone else's mouth.
What will slander do to me?

And Gulaim whipped the steed and the steed carried the evil
courier home. But some time later one of the proud suitors
appeared and said to Gulaim,

When I joke with you
You let go with a lash.
Would even the most malicious of mares
Kick a stallion till he's senseless?

The importunate suitors tried to enlist Gulaim's father's help,
but the proud young woman spurned them:

Having bared her teeth of pearls,
Gulaim flung him, like an enemy,
To her father's feet, saying,
"Take the young man
And start the *toy* without me!"
And she flew off to her island in a whirl.

The family had wished for Gulaim. They wanted a daughter
and she was born. From childhood they raised the little girl
in freedom. In the next stanza Gulaim reminisces about her
childhood in a conversation with her father:

> By the age of four
> You granted me a place of honor
> In your yurt[5]
> Equal to that of the eldest brother
> You intended me for a warrior,
> Seated me in a gold saddle,
> And the armor made of fine ringlets
> Gleamed brightly on me.
> And with a toy lance
> In my childlike hand, not yet grown strong,
> I learned in the meadow
> To catch up with my brothers at a run!

The images of Gulaim and her female comrades-in-arms, as well as a second heroine named Altynay, are, in their own way, the impetus for the establishment of Islam. Islam advocates seclusion for women, if not their total isolation from public life, something that Gulaim and her comrades did not experience or practice. Extremely significant in this respect is Altynay's bold and independent reply to Nadir the Shah's bid for her:

> I am free in my conduct.
> I am my own person.
> Why should I bow before you
> Like a blade of grass? . . .
> I will not become your wife
> And you are not so great that
> From our free steppes
> We should pay you taxes!

Altynay was also raised in freedom and as an equal to her twin brother. Both were of a Herculean build, and brother

5. A nomad's tent in Central Asia.

and sister were inseparable. They hunted together and
Altynay was just as ardent as her brother:

> Catching sight of a mountain goat
> She would flush with excitement.
> And it would happen at times
> That, with her bow and arrow drawn,
> Her evil *argamak*[6]
> Would buckle under her suddenly.

But there were envious people in Altynay's midst Evil lips
spreading abuse about her; black rumors emanated from the
palace:

> With her brother
> She is both sister and wife.
> She shares her bed with him!

It is Nadir the Shah whom she has spurned, and his slaves
spread the calumny; the people were not involved in the dissemination of these black rumors.

> Altynay gathered her flowing
> Black tresses into a knot
> And tucked it under her beaver *malakhai*[7]
> Brother embraced sister by the shoulders
> And led her to a woodland campfire.
> Such was her beauty,
> So chaste and pure!
> How vile was the slander!

The epic *Forty Maidens* is deeply poetic and sympathetic
to its heroines. The people's favorite daughters are raised to

6. A purebred horse.
7. A fur cap with large earflaps.

the stature of goddesses. Consider this description of a battle
with the enemy:

> Gulaim's forty falcons,
> Her forty bold friends,
> Beat the enemy back from forty sides.
> Forty blizzards accompany them
> And Azrael [8] serves them.
> A righteous judgment is accomplished.
> Forty pairs of silver wings—
> The sleeves of their battle shirts of mail—
> Tear the night into shreds.

After the *toy* the Asiatic amazons, tired and happy, bathe in
a stream:

> They untied their long tresses,
> Threw off their clothes, and entered
> Into the silver of the flowing waters.
> The gurgling freshets of water
> Opened up their rippled embraces to the maidens
> And washed the dust and sweat from them.

Isn't Sarbinaz made to look divine, the first to reveal Gulaim
the war leader's secret? "A foreign khan wants to plunder the
people," says Sarbinaz. "Take courage, friends! Gulaim has
instructed us in martial arts from the age of sixteen. None of
us must be a coward, otherwise it will mean our end!"

> Of forty maids
> The youngest was the
> Dark-complexioned Sarbinaz.
> Of forty young falcons

8. The Moslem angel of death.

The bravest was the young falcon
Sarbinaz.

In battle Sarbinaz is described even more sublimely:

With seven diamond wreaths on her head,
With the sun in her very eyes,
With sword in hand,
In armor of rainbow colors
Stands Sarbinaz!

Sometimes the images of the heroines take on a fairy-tale quality. In a difficult moment Altynay sings,

I was a fighter and I was burned in chains.
I was a palace and I was reduced to ashes.

A few words on the Kara-kalpak national character are in order. The Kara-kalpaks are related to the Pechenegi (the "black *klobuks*" [9] of Russian chronicles, *klobuk* corresponding to the Turkic word *kara-kalpak*, "black cap"). Written sources dating as far back as the sixteenth and seventeenth centuries reveal that separate groups of Kara-kalpaks were living at the basin of the lower Syr Darya River in the northeast and in the regions of the lower Emba and the Yaika Rivers (the Urals) in the northwest. They were also found along the shores of the Caspian Sea ("Astrakhan"). From the earliest times they lived along the Aral Sea and were occupied predominantly with agriculture as well as with the equally peaceful activity of fishing. When attacked from the outside, they were intractable and remained independent—their epic recounts this with passion. Gulaim, for example, renounces her brothers, who turned out to be cowards. Betrayal is a disgrace

9. The headgear of an Orthodox monk.

among the Kara-kalpak nation, and Gulaim therefore even refuses to commit her brothers' ashes to interment so they do not defile the earth.

The poem *Forty Maidens* has evidently withstood many changes as it passed from one narrator to another, and from generation to generation. One thing is beyond question: The story of Gulaim and her maiden-warriors and the courage of the Herculean Altynay contain elements that reflect an ancient way of life, particularly the epoch of the matriarchy. At that time, women not only were equal to men but often occupied a much higher position in the society. For the woman brought forth life and the importance of the role of the mother was never subject to any doubt. Gulaim becomes the ruler of her country and her power remains intact even when she marries. It is not she who goes to the homeland of the spouse, but he who remains in the land of the Kara-kalpaks. Another notable aspect of the poem is its progressiveness. To have created an image of a woman-warrior and a wise and just ruler is to remind people of the existence of good and truth even at a time when oppressive laws prevailed and were defended by feudal lords.

Gulaim is mighty, Altynay is majestic, and Sarbinaz, their younger friend, is decisive. Sarbinaz earns the love of her female comrades-in-arms through her exploits. In one scene she breaks through a hail of arrows to arrive as Gulaim's ambassador. Neither abuse nor threats from the enraged khan frighten her. Sarbinaz's words are full of virtue and irony:

> Hey you, Khan Surtayshan
> Shut your trap!
> I trample your power with my feet.
> Gulaim does not wish the people evil
> And did not come to your capitol for that reason.

Certainly, Gulaim is a noble warrior. She is a magnanimous adversary and the forty maidens are proud of their leader. She does not attack people like a robber as Surtayshan does. She even grants him seven days to prepare for single combat. Gulaim knows that truth is on her side and that seven days will not save the tyrant. And she does vanquish him. But after defeating the khan, Gulaim does not exhibit greed or vainglory, and she demands retribution only because the people expect it. Her vengeance is directed solely at the wicked despot and his companions.

The democratic motifs in the epic *Forty Maidens* may not have been inserted in the poem at the very beginning, for there existed a tacit censorship even for the singer-improvisers (*shairs*) under the power of the khans, lords, and Moslem clergy. Nevertheless, the optimistic essence of the poem remains and it speaks convincingly of the inner strength of the people and their undying spirit. And there is another related idea at the heart of this tale: No nation is another's enemy. The enemies are the bloodthirsty power seekers. Furthermore, animals assist the heroes of this epic: There are fast horses, birds, and even tigers. After all, Kara-kalpakya is not only desert and steppes but also lands that have long been irrigated, lakes, rivers, and plateaus where the mighty waters of the Amu Darya flow. In their infancy these waters broke into many canals and channels. Along their banks are swamps, often compared with the jungle, overgrown with thick tall rushes. Here one can encounter tigers. For hundreds of miles the azure waters of the Aral Sea, with its many islands, wash Kara-kalpakya. Miueli, the island on which the fortress is located, is described as "green curled" in the poem, full of fruit and flowers. The fullness of the land pervades every moment in the poem, even for instance when the young Sarbinaz guesses Gulaim's bold plans:

> And proud of her young friend
> Gulaim then embraced
> The sagacious Sarbinaz
> And placed a bunch of roses
> Into both of her dark-skinned hands,
> And kissing her on both cheeks
> Called her a sweet and clever person.
> She led her into her white yurt
> And there she seated her
> And she laid heaps of colorful
> Garments at her feet—
> Bright red and gold—
> And then they descended to the orchards
> To gather fruit for her.

Also full of tenderness are the lines describing Altynay's preparations for her final battle with Nadir the Shah, who had insulted the virtue of this splendid youth. In this next stanza Gulaim bestows gifts on Altynay:

> At dawn of this brightest of days
> Altynay received a fire-breathing steed.
> And the incomparable Gulaim put
> Shoes of morocco leather on her feet,
> Dressed her in six shirts of mail,
> Pleated her hair into a hundred braids,
> Brought her a sword and lance.

Incidentally, the women-warriors of this epic use swords, lances, and bows and arrows as their main weapons. They also participate in hand-to-hand fighting. The circle of friends underwent their training in the wide meadows for a serious purpose and the impending battle does not frighten them. After learning of the enemy attack, "Gulaim merely raised her pitch-black eyebrows like two wings," and a terrifying righteous anger illuminated her face.

> And the resplendent Gulaim
> Ordered her forty friends
> To saddle the swift steeds
> And to follow her
> To the mountains
> On a forty-day march.
> "Let the fat fall from the steeds!" she cried.

The next stanza contains the exciting tale of Gulaim and her beloved army avenging the enemy for the destruction and desecration of her people, those most beloved by her. Courage united with truth leads them to a victory over evil.

> The battle thundered for seven days and seven nights.
> And the battlefield became crowded with dead bodies.
> And for seven days and seven nights
> No one fed or watered the horses,
> Nor did they eat, drink, or sleep themselves.

The enemy camp is severely reduced, but Gulaim also suffers losses. Three of her friends are decapitated by the sword; seven are wounded by arrows. The young army is tired. The commander gives them a respite, but she herself cannot sleep:

> Gulaim the young woman-warrior
> Walked right up to the fortress itself
> And removing her helmet
> From her head
> Put her ear to the wall
> And heard in the silence
> The voice of her mother—

> The wail and the groan,
> The voice of her mother—
> The cry and the shout.

Gulaim rose and her heart filled with a thirst for victory greater
than before. The bitterness is not only in the voice of her
mother: The entire nation of Turkestan is crying. Gulaim summons her remaining friends to carry out a just reprisal against
the insidious enemy. And the young women find in themselves
new strength for a new battle. They defeat the foreign Khan,
for they are driven by a belief in the necessity of retribution.
This is their one single drive:

> With a shine in their fearless eyes
> How many lightning horsewomen
> Raise themselves up in their stirrups at once!
> The importance lies not in their names.

After the battle the young women force the destroyers to
compensate for the damage they inflicted on the native people.
But at the same time, the folk heroines are magnanimous.
After routing Nadir the Shah's troops, Gulaim calls for an end
to the war. "The people of Khorezm," she says, "are not our
enemies. We have rid them of their tyrant. That's enough!"
She does not require any innocent victims:

> Gulaim slid down from her saddle
> And surveyed the battlefield
> And keened over every corpse.
> Her tears fell.

She frees the captives and helps the wounded:

> She poured the balsam of love
> On their weary hearts.

The epic *Forty Maidens* can be compared to *The Song of Roland* and Od the Beauty to Gulaim. Doubtless every nation has a need for heroes, for courageous characters capable of defending good against the forces of evil.

The following is some historical information for those interested in the relations between Central Asia and Russia. The annexation of the land of the Kara-kalpaks by the Russian Empire occurred only in the second half of the nineteenth century. At that time a law calling for the abolition of slavery in the Khiva Khanate in Central Asia was issued. And despite the dominating role of the greater power over the lesser nations, perhaps one ought to agree with Friedrich Engels, who wrote Karl Marx on May 23, 1851: "Russia is indeed playing a progressive role with respect to the East ... Russia's dominion is having a civilizing effect on the Black and Caspian Seas and on Central Asia." The same can be said of the West's influence on Russia. Both Peter the Great and Catherine the Great (Russia's most celebrated leaders) understandably turned to Europe for the good of Russia: European culture is older and has proved more stable throughout the years. Ancient Greece also exerted an influence that is perceptible and tangible.

Many outdated customs have survived to the present day in Central Asia. And the bureaucratic apparatus, highly developed throughout the Soviet Union, has slowed the advancement of the Turkic people on a cultural level. Most often it is the sons of upper-echelon party members who study in larger cities. As a rule people from this level do not become reformers concerned with the circumstances of ordinary people. But on the whole, the situation in Central Asia is better than that of the Turkic people beyond our borders, where the influence of Islam makes society more conservative and less flexible, effects most directly felt by women.

Translated by Rebecca Park

Women, Birth, and Children

The special role of women in reproduction has been acknowledged in Soviet legislation. Free health care combined with liberal maternity leave provisions (112 days at full pay, partially paid leave for a year after) are highly progressive by U.S. standards. Recent legislation seeks to encourage larger families (the birth rate among Russians is quite low) by giving one-time grants of 50 to 100 rubles for each child, providing more liberal leave for the care of sick children (open to fathers as well), and reducing child care fees for large families.

As the essays in this section indicate, the reality is too often short of the ideal. Although the Soviets pioneered the introduction of "painless childbirth" techniques popularized in the West by Fernand Lamaze, institutional rigidity and the lack of resources can make childbirth a painful nightmare. Fearful of infection, the Soviets bar fathers or other relatives from maternity hospitals for seven to ten days before and after the birth. Prenatal education is minimal at best; overworked staff do little to prepare new mothers; overcrowding and callousness are too common. Rising infant mortality statistics indicate that state military spending priorities are having an effect on the quality of health care.

Similarly, although Soviet legislation about child care is exemplary, the facilities cannot satisfy demand in all areas. There is no waiting list in Moscow, but in Uzbekistan, even by 1990, only one third of all children will have spaces in child care centers.

For those who do not want children, conditions are difficult. Birth control pills are not approved for large-scale distribution; diaphragms are hard to find and often don't fit properly; Soviet condoms are aptly called "galoshes" and in extremely short supply. Lacking other alternatives, Soviet women resort to abortion. Although abortion is legal and free, it is subject to the same problems of overcrowding and indifferent and sometimes incompetent staff that afflict the health care system as a whole.

91

An Uphill Battle

KARI UNKSOVA
Leningrad, Russia

Dedicated to my daughter

"Mama, if a perfect person looks in the mirror and wishes that it would be covered with roses, will it be covered or not?"

"It will be covered, my child."

"No, it won't, because if they're perfect, then they won't wish for such a thing. And if they do wish for it, then at that point they stop being perfect."

"Good Lord," said her father when I related his daughter's words to him. "Good Lord," he said imitating her low, slow contralto. "How many people live out their lives without even getting to the question, never mind to an answer."

The child had just turned six. And it was then, for the first time, as I recall, that I felt someone's invisible, powerful hand lift ever so slightly the load under which I dragged myself around all those years, from as far back as the day after conception, when the tough fingers of endless nausea squeezed my throat and a wave of repulsive smells gushed over me. They seemed like dense impenetrable balls, pieces of gelatin that I was swallowing instead of air.

I had just graduated from the university. My position with respect to an assignment was unclear. They assigned me to Krasnoyarsk and my husband to Norilsk, but neither of us went to these classic resorts for convicts. My husband had been the more brilliant student and was invited to stay on and study in a graduate program, and I was physically unable to go where I had been assigned. A peaceable divisional police inspector used to visit us in the mornings and remind us of our civic duty. I did not have a job and neither did my husband. True, we did have money from our parents, both his and mine. Finally, the director of a quasi-scientific institute with whom we were acquainted took pity on a pregnant woman and took me in. For this kindness he endured prolonged harassment over the telephone from university officials and from Moscow, for the authorities had received malicious, gloating denunciations of me and my husband. We were black sheep and only by sheer force of talent did we stay safely within the boundaries of the university. An anonymous letter with an especially nasty complaint arrived at my alma mater before my documents for admittance. In about two months, when I had already begun to forget the names of my close friends under the blissful and sleepy idiocy that flooded over me in the intervals between exhausting attacks of retching (lasting approximately an hour, or an hour and a half at most), when I began to feel a small elongated apple over my lap, everything somehow began to settle down. In April, during a bright period, I locked myself away to work. (Why, I now wonder bitterly. The food did not do me any good. Better to have gone hungry, or at least have gone to the dacha and let myself and the child breathe in peace.) This is hard to explain without knowing our idiosyncrasies. My mother-in-law and mother and father, being people of different origins and positions in life, were equally slavish in their adherence to the idea of the state system, as has been all of Russia from time immemorial. Our artificial city Peter grew like a dwarf on that idea and it was in us also.[1] To not work? The very idea of not working would never occur to anyone, even though for a pregnant woman to work is absolute vivisection for both the woman and the child, aggravated by the barbaric

1. The "city Peter" refers to Leningrad, originally named St. Petersburg. It was built in 1703 on the order of Peter the Great.

binding control of the district—or, I should say, the quadrant
—doctor, whoever he or she happens to be.[2] Mine was an in-
sane old woman who did not remember her own words or me
or even the scheduled checkups, which she sometimes tried to
carry out twice or forgot to conduct altogether. In a panic she
would wail that I must be taken immediately to the emergency
hospital, but by morning she would refuse to sign my sick slip.
In addition, she tried to understate the length of my pregnancy,
to deprive me of the pitiful crumbs provided by the state—a
two-month stipend, the minimum, since I had just started my
job. The senior nurse who compiled the pages of documenta-
tion needed to authorize my future criminal idleness was the
same sort. I encountered not one single kind or caring word
in that accursed clinic—only analyses, smears, blood tests, blood
pressure (mine was catastrophically low and my headaches were
so intense that I could only see darkness, but this did not worry
anyone: They just neatly recorded the data and left it at that).
In the mornings I would squeeze into an overcrowded trolley
in which sweat, cheap perfume, every kind of male and female
odor, and the smell of peeling paint and rotting rubber sickened me. If I did not jump off in the middle of a trip in order
to run to the nearest ditch, I rode the trolley almost to the
harbor where the air was fresher and smelled only of leather
from a warehouse. If the wind was blowing from the direction
of the town, it still smelled incredibly bad. There I worked in
a room that I shared with four doctoral candidates and my
supervisor, a small fat man, irascible and given to fussing, who

2. In the Soviet health care system each person is assigned to a doctor at a
clinic in the district in which he or she lives or works. In pre-revolutionary
Russia supervisors were assigned to various quadrants of a city. Their
function was to observe the activities of people living within their quadrant and to report them to the police department. By substituting the
adjective "quadrant" for "district" the author implies that district doctors
carry out the same functions of surveillance as the pre-revolutionary supervisors.

did not attempt to seem fair or even correct but who, for some
reason, liked me and Lyuda, the lab assistant. The work tables
stood next to one another. The windows faced north; a ray of
sunshine never appeared in the room, but at least there was
light. In the basement my husband and I occupied after my
parents left for their co-op apartment, a Khruschev-era slum,
there was no light: An electric light shone day and night and
the basement smelled of rats.

My husband and I were young and we loved each other
deeply. We lived on our own almost all the time, which was a
great good fortune. We were not forced to sleep in the same
room with a mother or mother-in-law as were most of our
classmates. We were not forced to endure the misery of living
in a dormitory and the constant worry about our daily bread.
We had friends. So a year went by, then another, then a third,
and an end finally came to the graduate program. We were
earning average but decent money and we had interesting research. And there was always the symphony, the ballet which
I loved, books, and records—all in all, a sensible life. Had
anyone told me that at the age of forty torn underwear would
still be a regular problem for me, that we would barely save
our child's life, that my husband would never finish any master's program, that we would both bid farewell to this regular
life, that we would bid farewell to books, the theater, friends,
research and, finally, to the fatherland in which we would live
like foreigners from an unknown and superfluous Palestine,
that our cherished silver would be trashed in a pawn shop and
our daughter would be in and out of hospitals, sanitariums,
and boarding schools—had anyone told me that back then!

They should have, they should have. But the story cannot
be put down all at once. I am sitting in Moscow, and that is
not by chance. I am in Moscow, in the Tekstilshchik section
(to reach that area requires a subway ride and then a transfer
to a bus)—dirty truck depots, high-voltage wires depressingly
creeping up to the searchlights. The searchlights mercurially

aim over the multilayered mess—fences of cement blocks, wooden barracks, pipes, cranes, dirty snow, the beginning of March. It looks like there will not be a war; we have resigned ourselves to Afghanistan, little by little the funerals creep by. A homeless boxer dog roams the streets; there are many jackdaws in Moscow. Still I breathe easier here. The same old dirty kitchen wall studded with knife marks, a cockroach with a new shell climbs along a crack. The door of the wardrobe presses crookedly against the bed. A mop stretching across the kitchen floor props up the refrigerator door. The door handle broke. Surprising.

This is terrifying at first, but along the way there are plenty of other concerns. My husband went off on a research trip after passing his exams with superior marks, while I began to take walks at lunch time religiously and to walk home after work, which occupied two hours or more of my time. Through childlike foolishness I would buy all sorts of rubbish and end up dragging home a rather heavy load. I do not know how to wander idly, although I write poetry. I take notice of nature only indirectly, through a peripheral vision, and I do so precisely and acutely. Somehow I do not get impressions directly. They put me in a stupor. I fall asleep, become unconscious.

Childhood wore me out with pleasure—the bright shades of green and the blue sky. When at age thirteen I began to write poetry, the first and most saddening result was the loss of this furious range of colors. The more I tried to capture it and fix it on the page, the more obliquely nature behaved, slipping off into some kind of light ether, elusive to sight and feelings. First there was nostalgia; then the gray, almost colorless world became habit. I should have known that in this world the more attention I pay to my senses, experiences, and interrelationships, the farther I stray from my soul, which is like a green leaf.

In the happy period of my pregnancy all the joy of colors returned to me. In my sleepy stupefaction I felt firmly the powerful force of the blue sky, prominent green lawns, sharp black of wires. Pigeons were big and fat. Cats smelled and lived their wild lives. I hardly saw any human beings and had little need of them. The thirst to look and to keep on looking gripped me. But I do not remember where I was living at the time. I have the vague feeling that it was with my parents. I remember that I smelled cigarettes on the street from the fourth floor. I smoked and rather a lot, but now smoking is repulsive to me as is the very sight of cigarettes. I remember that for some reason my sister turned up at our place, but I have completely forgotten how and when this move transpired. We were expecting a daughter. The whole family was certain that that is how it would turn out. It seemed to me that I would have nothing to say to a little boy, but I would pass on everything to a daughter—and how much there was! I was such a know-it-all for my twenty-four years.

The baby girl's character began to reveal itself rather early. She barely had time to move before I felt a certain lack of contact with her, arising from a difference in our natures. In a letter to my husband I complained of her introvertedness, stubbornness, and rationality, of how reserved she was, of her intense concentration and the absence of a lively mind. But what grieved me most of all was the total lack of that easiness, that adaptability and liveliness that so help in life.

The totally alien being within me turned over stubbornly and with difficulty, striving especially to shove my liver, which became so painful that it did not give me peace day or night. It came time to go on maternity leave. Something stirred in my parents and my father took me and my sister to Gagra.[3] There I lolled about in the nude on the women's beach almost until the birth.

---

3. A Black Sea resort in the Caucasus, thirty-seven miles south of Sochi. It is in the Abkhazian Autonomous Region of Georgia.

My parents were obsessed with the idea that my pregnancy and the birth of my child should in no way alter their egalitarian attitude toward me and my sister. I am giving birth, but my sister has dermatitis and an unhappy lonely life (she had separated from her husband at that time). To sacrifice to an abstract idea, a spontaneous impulse—how like us all that is, how much in our blood it is! I sunbathed and tanned and swam. Gagra smelled of boxwood. At night my sister exasperated me by forbidding me to open the *fortochka*[4] in the narrow closet of a room we were renting, and I would sit and suffocate. When I finally fell asleep, I would dream that my deceased grandmother was raining pine needles on me. We were fed poorly in the restaurant and I continued to vomit even though I was in the late stages of pregnancy. Georgians impudently looked over Russian "blondes" from head to toe on the way to the beach. On top of everything, acquaintances arrived and I had to make conversation with them. I had nothing to talk about. Everything was unimportant. Music grated on my ears, I did not feel like reading books, and in the cinema I could not remember the face flitting across the screen.

On October 10, we returned to "Peter." We were met at the airport with fur coats. It was snowing. As we landed, the stewardess passed through the cabin handing out little cases for our ball point pens—ink could leak from them—and suddenly I was seized with a momentary terror. I had a clear vision that in the defenseless little body locked within me capillaries were bursting and dangerous shifts of body fluids were taking place. Even now I am convinced that this flight caused the child irreparable damage. Something became displaced in my daughter's brain, some sort of short circuit that made itself known long after that.

4. A small hinged windowpane that opens for ventilation.

Then we went back to the basement which needed repairs. We did not have money for these and we hired a strange little man who was working on a construction site. For all three rooms, the corridor, and the kitchen he charged us about thirty rubles. In addition he covered one of the rooms with a careful layer of spackle. It smelled for almost ten years afterward but the surface turned out beautifully. Everything was painted with textured brush strokes, lively and energetic, a slightly yellowish, natural shade. He swiped drying oil, cement, alabaster, and spackle from the construction site in huge cans, carrying on what has been the custom in our blessed fatherland for the past three hundred years. People keep looting everything, but they cannot manage to loot it all. Russian peasants never had any property and they always related to state property on their own terms. They called our craftsman Ivan Yelenova[5] because he was just like a character in an operetta. He did repairs for us for almost half a year but he did finally finish them. After every meal, which was accompanied by a "short,"[6] he requested a raise and stopped working for a while. Finally, we stopped feeding him and he meekly ate a cafeteria schnitzel with his fingers in the corner of the room. He would wipe his mouth with his hand and then set about his work, telling endless stories about his shitty wife who beat him on Saturdays. On Saturday and Sunday he tried to stretch out his hours, practically until 1:00 A.M. He would come back at 7:00 in the morning after probably having spent what remained of the night wandering the streets.

When he tore off the wallpaper, he made a mess of the furniture, littered the place with plaster, stacked books and pictures in messy heaps, and covered them with oilcloth. My husband washed my feet—I had long been unable to bend over—and hoisted me onto our couch, which had sunken in. Glanc-

5. Yelenova is a feminine patronymic.
6. A 250-gram bottle of vodka.

ing around at the surroundings he said, "Just the right time
to give birth—in these unsanitary conditions." Earlier on the
same day I had gone to the clinic and my old crow doctor had
gathered her students around and lectured them, "Look at
her. Her stomach is extended way up high. It's putting pressure on her diaphragm. Look how heavily she breathes; she
won't deliver soon. It'll be approximately two or three more
weeks." But I already felt a tightness in my side, which I complained about. The old crow glanced at me for half a second
and said, "Will you get yourself home, my little child. You
won't be giving birth today or tomorrow." Deceived by the
night blindness of Doc Crow, the exhibit stepped lively all the
way home where she went to drag books and all sorts of junk
from one place to another.

Night fell and I fell asleep. But at 2:30 A.M. something
jolted me. I woke up and looked at the clock. A sense of alarm
pounded within me; the feeling was like that before a thun-
derstorm. I sensed my own unimportance. It is difficult to
convey this feeling of smallness, of the earth becoming un-
reliable, as if you could blow away and there was nothing to
catch hold of. The sheet was wet and people had to be called.

I knocked on the wall but my husband did not wake up.
The terror grew in me like a roaring avalanche and, thank
God, my sister woke up and came running. She ran to call the
ambulance and to wake up my husband. Otherwise, in my
madness I would have walked off, following my nose, and God
only knows how things might have turned out.

I smile when I remember how we leafed through the Czech-
oslovakian manual on childbirth and child rearing that we had
obtained with difficulty. I remember how much difficulty we
had understanding that water was coming out of me, and how
I sent my husband to the phone when the contractions began
but when they stopped, I begged him not to call anyone. It is
better to give birth at home under unsanitary conditions than

to end up in an emergency hospital as a regular patient. I would not wish that on my worst enemy.

But the ambulance arrived and they loaded me into the vehicle, and my husband with me. Everything happened so fast that I do not remember where I gave birth. I think it was on Vasilyevsky Island.[7]

The hell started in the isolation unit, where a furious nurse shouted at my husband, shouted at me, and performed a series of procedures that were not only humiliating but so brutal that I felt like a prisoner at Mauthausen. After throwing a pair of scissors at me to cut my nails, she set about washing the examining table and bedpan after me. The old hag of a doctor on duty conducted an extremely painful examination and then wondered why groans and other sounds extraneous to the examination were coming from me. Then they put everything onto a stretcher and carted me off to the delivery room. There was no time left. I had no time for anything. From time immemorial women in our family have given birth quickly. I was thinking that would not be the case with me. Physical education classes had always been a trial for me. All my life I have never been muscular; my body was soft and weak. I could not climb a rope, do exercises on the parallel bars, run fast, or jump high.

It was only at the moment of giving birth that I realized that this process requires a completely different kind of strength—the strength of an inner enthusiasm, an instantaneous concentration bordering on madness, that ecstatic strength which catapults crazy people up six-meter walls.

They say everyone has his or her own threshold of pain. My feebleness has long been a terrible cross for me: I fear pain

7. A large island, part of the city of Leningrad, includes many historic institutions such as the university and the Academy of Sciences, as well as residential areas. Some of the city's newest and most fashionable apartment blocks are on this island.

and I have my reasons for that. Within two minutes from the moment I injure a finger my scalp is crawling. The reaction is instantaneous and terrible. Everything from my toenails to my hair hurts and I no longer know what the original source of pain was. Novocain and other such remedies do not act on me or else they act several hours later.

The so-called lightning births—and mine was exactly that —are not good for either mother or the child. They are fraught with the possibilities of hemorrhaging, ruptures, and eclampsia.[8] If the mother is emotionally unstable and requires special benevolent attention from physicians, where is it?

In that same hell, where the pain surpasses all limit so that when they cut you alive with scissors, you hear only the crunch and you do not feel any additional torture, in that same hell, only the squeamish shouts of the doctors, who were of no help to me whatsoever, invaded. "Shame on you," they screamed at me, "an educated woman and you're screaming like some old hag!" I remember that even in my delirium a ripple of laughter passed through me as I thought, "Curious how they can recognize education in this unbelievable creature writhing about on this narrow stretcher." This was not a scream but something totally otherworldly. "Can this really be me?" was the thought that flitted through what once was my brain.

"Yeah, hold her down," said a male physician maliciously.

I remember the expression of one old nurse; it is etched like a photograph in my mind. It did not reveal so much of her own pity as a learned, job-related pity. Still it revealed at least some kind of pity and it will be with me forever. She approached me and took my hand into her own, and her hand gave me a soft smoldering warmth. The pain abated instantly. And the several seconds of calm and gratitude allowed me to gather my strength and realize what was going on around me.

---

8. A form of toxemia during pregnancy characterized by convulsions.

The old woman is probably dead by now. For the likes of her, the earth will be a feather bed; she will rest easy in her grave.

"When did the delivery process begin?"

"Last name?" (Is it not already written down on the little card?)

"Year of birth?"

"When did it begin?"

God, how terrible to be a nameless woman giving birth among strangers.

"Last name?"

"When did it begin?"

With lips that could barely move I answered them, naming the time over and over again which, as luck would have it, I had memorized.

"You're lying."

"When did it begin?"

"Write whatever you want," I said when I could no longer answer their questions.

"Some kind of nut, this woman."

"Yeah, some kind of nut."

"We'll have to operate."

I heard the crunch of the scissors, and finally the contractions started. Then there was no more pain, and the entire body receded into an unbelievable strain.

"Open your eyes."

"Don't close your eyes."

There are no eyes; there is no face; there is nothing.

"It's a boy, it's a boy, it's a boy."

"Not on your life!" fiercely flitted through my mind.

I remembered that I had to look for myself and whatever I would see is what the baby would be.

"Ahhhh." That was the sound with which my gaze met the little baby, a blue beast in some kind of white putty with a powerful cable of an umbilical cord, striking in its length and

thickness. I saw a face, the face in portraits of Beethoven when
he had gone completely deaf. It was concentrated and puffy,
with a mane of tousled wet hair, and it hung from its chin in
the physician's hand which wore a tight yellow glove drenched
in blood up to the elbow. Nearby was a mountain of pulsing
placenta, which drew from me an awesome feeling of respect
for its mountainous pile of powerful blood vessels and capillaries. It had an air of protection and strength about it. They
wheeled me out into the corridor and forgot about me for a
long time. Then they sewed me back up, carted me off to the
ward, and threw me on the bed where I fell into a deep,
blissful sleep.

They say about birth, "The hill is steep, but easy to forget."
And this is so. Nothing but bright memories about a deed
well done remain from that hellish pain. But the insult will
be with me forever. Who do you have to be in order not to
feel the pitiless indifference of the hands of strangers, the
filthy crudeness (they did not fail to remark, of course, for
what deed I was paying when I gave birth), the indifference
to the mother and to the child. Such indifference when the
most terrifying helplessness comes over a woman giving birth
is fundamentally contrary to nature. Midwives, where are you?

Translated by Rebecca Park

A Few More Words on the Subject
of Free Medical Treatment

VALENTINA LEFTINOVA
Moscow, Russia

In the Leningrad newspaper *Smena*, I happened upon a selection called "Return from across the Ocean." It was a letter to the editor signed "M. Budilov, Sailor." The letter described a waitress who worked on the ship *Mikhail Lermontov*, which was making a trip across the Atlantic Ocean. Due to the effects of a rough storm, she gave birth to her child prematurely in a hospital in the United States. They placed her in a very good hospital, "in the most expensive ward," and even assigned her a nurse who spoke Russian, since the mother did not speak any foreign languages. She spent a month in the hospital before the ship, which in the meantime had made a return voyage to the U.S.S.R., came back and picked her up. The American women who worked in the hospital were surprised that our government assumed complete responsibility for the expenses incurred during her stay. The letter closed with the words, "No, not every American can afford such a stay. Elvira's stay cost $20,000. That surprised us sailors, who have grown used to another way of life."

This article is not unusual in the least. Articles of similar content appear periodically in the pages of our press. For example, articles describe how Soviet sailors saved a foreign fisherman, lavished care and attention on him, and provided him with medical treatment absolutely free of charge, whereas in his own country the same treatment would have cost him a large sum and so on. Evidently such articles are required on a regular basis to remind the reader of the advantages of the Soviet way of life.

As deplorable as this is, these articles achieve their goal from time to time. The idea that we really do have some advantages over the West is involuntarily absorbed by the mind of the reader, especially the sort of reader who does not reflect on the matter seriously. And this occurs in spite of the fact that the reader has repeatedly experienced the poor quality and bureaucratic approach of free medical treatment enjoyed by "the simple folk." (I will not undertake to pass judgment on the medical facilities available to our privileged personages but closed to the ordinary worker.)

There is no question about it; free medical care is a good service. Expensive medical care is inhumane. But anyone can see that it is better to have good medical care that is costly than bad medical service that is free. Our people realized this long ago and, to the degree possible, now turn to private practitioners who treat patients for a fee. (As a rule, these doctors also work in government institutions, concealing their private practice from the authorities and thereby avoiding a high rate of taxation. This is especially true of pediatricians. Many women I know prefer to have their children treated by private doctors with good reputations than by a district doctor, and women usually recommend doctors to one another. If we accept free medical care, we do not have the right to choose our own doctor. We have to limit ourselves to the services of one certain district doctor, who is assigned to a patient according to where he or she works or lives, even if the patient happens not to trust this doctor for good reason.) Thus the advantages of our form of medical service over that of the West are extremely suspect.

As far as the article with which we began is concerned, one cannot rule out the possibility that nothing described in it ever really took place, or that all the events took place entirely

differently. But let us assume that the entire article is the absolute truth. Now, let the question be asked clearly: Why was
it necessary to keep this woman in an expensive hospital, in
the most expensive ward, for an entire month? I presume she
could have received high-quality medical care elsewhere in the
United States (especially when you compare it to what she
would have received here in our country) for substantially less
money.

One of the reasons for this stay (if in fact it really did take
place) may have been the opportunity it offered our government to show clearly how our society takes care of people. Yet
we know very well that this expensive hospital stay has nothing in common with how women giving birth are treated in
our society. If you also bear in mind that our government
does not even have enough foreign currency to meet minimal
needs (in particular, for the purchase of a sufficient quantity
of imported medicines and medical equipment), then anyone
can see that the squandering of "the people's wealth" on a
wildly extravagant propaganda show has nothing to do with
the true quality of medical care people receive.

Translated by Rebecca Park

The Other Side of the Coin

NATASHA MALTSEVA
Arkhangelsk, Russia

The greatest good that nature has intended for woman is for her to fulfill her purpose as a mother. Only a woman who experiences the feeling of motherhood is capable of understanding and valuing the singular responsibility for the life of a tiny infant. It is not without reason that there is a prize medal in the Soviet Union called Mother-Heroine.[1]

But this article concerns the so-called single mother, the woman who takes on the brave task of bearing and bringing up a child without a father. What moves her to take such a desperate step?

Many women who resolve to follow this courageous road do not always have an idea of the thorny path they have chosen. There are women who do not even have any close relatives or parents who could help them during this difficult time.

Nor can these women expect much help or support from society. The government allots twenty rubles a month for the support of an illegitimate child. Mothers must obtain these twenty rubles by going through numerous formalities and humiliations. No one will tell them that they have a right to this financial support; no one will send any notices to their homes. And worse, it is impossible to survive even for a week on this ridiculous amount. The single woman with a child and no one to count on except herself must have a means of subsistence for at least one year.

Only a woman who has thoroughly thought over and antici-

---

1. The expression "the other side of the coin" is literally "the other side of the medal" in Russian.

pated all the difficulties of the single life, and has saved a certain amount of money before her child's birth, can live carefree for a year without working. Not many women are capable of doing this.

And what about those women who have not thought any of this through and have not taken any precautions for themselves for the year ahead? Only through extraordinary efforts are these women able to maintain a life for themselves, which also means a life for their children, the future members of society. But this society does not trouble itself with thinking about what is hidden in the depths of the loudly trumpeted slogan "the emancipated woman." No one thinks about the price that a woman has paid for what is called freedom.

Thus, a woman brings up her child to the age of one. Then, of course, she must count on the state day care centers to carry on her work. But here is a new problem: How does she get her child into one of these centers? In order to do this she must get on a waiting list at the center even before the birth of her child. There is one other way out: She can leave her job and get hired by the center; then they will accept her child. But if she does not have a college medical education, she will have to do the dirtiest and heaviest work, and at the same time take care of her own child.

Children's day care centers and nursery schools are the most destructive institutions in the U.S.S.R.'s health care system. The personnel of the institutions basically consist of middle-aged and elderly women. A small percentage are young women who work as cleaning ladies for the sake of being near their children. The majority of the middle-aged and elderly women do not have children of their own. It is hard to say what brings these older women to this wonderful flower garden of children's purity and spontaneity. But they hardly come with a feeling of self-sacrifice and self-denial for the sake of these weak, defenseless little babies who need a great deal of care.

There is one nurse and one nanny for every twenty-five to thirty children. These women must have tremendous patience and love in order to be able to meet their little charges with a smile and patiently care for them all day long, and then come to work again the next day with a fresh supply of emotional strength.

Very few women are capable of performing this heroic task. Most of them are guided by mercenary aims. They know that these tiny, defenseless creatures will tell no one about the things they silently witness, since they are not able to understand and judge the actions of adults. The children's lives are in the hands of the adults, who in turn take advantage. I have had occasion to be with these people, and have never met people more cruel and troublesome. They go to the day care centers with one thought in mind: to steal. They take away the children's food, their mainstay in life, and extend the meat with bread, thanks to meals that some clever cook invented, such as hamburgers, meatballs, dumplings and chopped beef. They also water down the sour cream and milk—that is convenient, too.

The sanitarium season, when children are sent out of the city to camps or dachas so that they may enjoy fresh air, fruits, and vegetables, also gives these corrupt people an opportunity to make a profit.

The staff members take the fruit that parents bring for their children, and divide it among themselves. They leave cookies, candies, and other sweets for the children, which are certainly not good for their health.

The nurses' hygienic care of the children is completely out of hand and very poor. Little girls are washed very rarely and are dried either with their own nightgowns or with one towel that is used for all children.

I recall that in the summer of 1976, at a dacha in Berngardovka, the children's infirmary was overflowing. The children were ill with severe respiratory diseases, lung complications, mumps, and dysentery. The ambulances knew the route to the infirmary very well, since they came there almost every day.

Thus, after a sanitarium season like this, the single mother who has entrusted her baby to a state institution is left with one alternative. She must rack her brains for another place to send her child for the summer.

The reason for such a state of affairs in all preschool institutions must be sought in the Soviet health care system and the management of personnel. The shortage of workers and the high turnover rate are caused by low wages. Nurses get eighty to ninety rubles a month; orderlies earn seventy-five rubles.[2]

But in the Soviet Union, a person has the right to choose. If the burdens of life with a child are too much for you, you can decide not to have a child. Abortions are officially allowed in the Soviet Union. Just ten or fifteen minutes (this is how long the operation takes) is all you need to be free of all the worry and annoyance connected with having a child.

But what emotional torments and physical sufferings these few minutes cost! I believe that most women who have experienced this inhuman torture even once would refuse to undergo this barbaric operation if they had normal, human conditions in which to live. Yet it is still not clear to society why a woman chooses to have an abortion. Sometimes, when a woman checks into a hospital and fills out the numerous papers needed to obtain an abortion, she is asked why she does not want to have the child. The answer, as a rule, is usually the same: She does not have normal living conditions or her pay is too low to support a child. Where this information is then transmitted is a mystery. We do not even know if it goes anywhere at all! At any rate, our "humane" society has done all that is possible,

---

2. According to the official exchange rate, $1.00 equals sixty-four kopecks. There are one hundred kopecks in a ruble.

and the "emancipated" Soviet woman fully senses her freedom in the most diverse ways.

If a woman has made up her mind to have an abortion, she is in for a "round of tortures." It starts with the humiliation of the gynecologist's exam, after which she must gather up a pile of papers for the coming execution, where she will be talked to with unconcealed scorn. To this the degradation of the last stages is added, through which the woman must pass en route to her destination. Then she must wait in line for an appointment. In a huge waiting room, almost without any light or air, women with worried and depressed faces sit on benches placed along the wall. They must sit for one and a half to two hours.

Thus, one hour follows another, and finally the woman comes closer to the torture fate has destined for her—that is, she ends up in an abortion clinic. The abortion clinic on Lermontov Prospekt is a monstrous institution—a slaughter-house, as women themselves call it. The treatment capacity of the clinic is two hundred to three hundred women patients a day.

In the clinic are huge rooms with ten to fifteen beds made up with flannel blankets. There are never enough sheets to go around, and the women must resort to various innovations in order to get by with just one sheet, by using it either as a cover or as an undersheet. And all this takes place in a medical institution, where surgery is performed on people.

But the women who come to this clinic do not pay any attention to these discomforts. They are seized with the horror of waiting for the impending blasphemy. Finally, the moment of decision arrives. The women are put in lines in front of the operating room. Two and sometimes six women are operated on at the same time. The operating tables are placed in such a way that the women who are waiting can see everything that is happening to the women who have gone before them. They can see the faces distorted in torment and the bloody mess flowing out of the women's wombs.

There are two doctors and one nurse in the operating room. The nurse says, "Quickly now, quickly!" The woman, who is shaking from fear and worry, is perched on the operating table, her movements awkward and unsure. The doctor tells her irritably what position she should assume on the table.

Finally, the woman is arranged and the doctor begins the operation. Sometimes she is given a shot but she does not feel its effect, since very little Novocain is injected and not enough time goes by for it to take effect. Consequently, since there is no anesthetic, the woman experiences terrible pain. Some women even lose consciousness. The nurse, who is waiting on two doctors at once, does not have time to help the patient. With difficulty, the patient is "brought back to her senses" and then led from the operating room. She is left outside with the women still waiting their turn, who take her back to her room. There, the woman writhes in pain for an hour or an hour and a half; she is nauseated to death, and sometimes vomits. The next day she is signed out, without anyone examining her general condition. She is left to hope for the best.

Medical care in the Soviet Union is based on the patient's ability to pull through, and has only a charitable function. The patients are given first aid, but after that they must rely exclusively on themselves.

Translated by Catherine A. Fitzpatrick

Upbringing

Young Soviets share the almost universal experience of receiving their earliest socialization in the family. As they grow older, they are more likely than their counterparts in the U.S. to be placed in the care of others, usually at one of the state-run child care centers. Soviet child care centers compare favorably with those in the U.S. in terms of availability and type of facilities, although demand still exceeds supply. Child care centers generally provide one hot meal a day, have a nurse on duty, and have separate nap rooms. As in the U.S., staff is generally low paid and children are more susceptible to sickness in these group situations.

From their earliest years in day care, Soviet children learn the importance of the collective. This can have positive results in teaching sharing and sensitivity to others, but as is noted by several of the feminist authors, it can also encourage a stifling conformity. Soviet children begin school at age seven. The schools' long hours, strict discipline, extensive homework, and emphasis on rote memorization would enthrall back-to-basics advocates. But Soviet teachers must adhere strictly to centrally mandated lesson plans that discourage creativity in them and their students.

Traditional values remain strong, despite the noticeable absence of formal religion as a major socializing force. For example, in terms of sex roles, studies of Soviet textbooks and children's literature indicate heavy reinforcement of traditional sex-role stereotypes. Popular beliefs about differences between the sexes are widely held, and as Mironova points out, these create barriers to Soviet women's sense of their own strengths and career choices.

How We Learned about Tatyana Larina

NADEZHDA ZOTOVA
Sverdlovsk, Urals, Russia

They say that girls today are not wise enough and have no pride; they are instead empty-headed. Actually, that might be true. But the whole problem is this: Whose fault is it? There is no question that every young person, every young woman, is responsible for herself, for her actions. But there must be *something* that precedes these actions. It simply is not fair to dump all the blame on an inexperienced person who is just starting out in life. There are definite circumstances in everyday life that play a large role in the formation of a young girl's character.

In former times, the governesses took care of young ladies' education and saw to it that young women acquired the proper tastes, views, and ideas. The result was that the majority of young ladies were like heroines in romantic novels—as a rule, absolutely passive and concerned only with getting married. A lady would secretly fantasize that a hussar would abduct her and carry her away. Girls from simple, lower-class families did not even know how to read or write and were married off at an early age, often against their will.

Nowadays, of course, it is a different story. Girls are educated in schools and people with a higher education teach them. Now other books interest the modern girl, not just novels. But here is the perplexing thing: The girls today read all sorts of trash. Yet they more or less love literature and art—these fields have been close to women's hearts from time immemorial. I say this not only on the strength of tradition but also because a woman's nature is more responsive, of greater emotional depth, and more artistic than that of a man. Therefore, an education in the humanities is particularly important for a girl. Schools should help a girl to develop depth of feeling, readiness, and an understanding of creativity (her own and others). But our lessons in school do not bring us any closer to literature. Students are not taught to perceive the books in a fresh and clear way, but rather are filled with clichés, which only serve to alienate them from what we "learn" in school. During our school days, we grow cold toward the classics, and many of us never return to them after we graduate. It has become popular to choose things that can be read in one sitting—if not newspapers, then detective novels, the Soviet version of the dime novel. Of course, the classics do not reflect our reality, but at least they are more relevant than detective stories, because they deal with questions of timeless import to humankind—questions of the deeper interrelationships in life. Pushkin was not a feminist, but his heroine Tatyana Larina was the personification of what was best in young women's souls at that time. Pushkin's talent enabled him to intuitively present the life of this woman, and Tatyana Larina could surprise us with her inner richness if we did *not* study the poem "Eugene Onegin" in the following manner.

Usually, we were assigned several chapters to read for homework—either chapters from the work itself or from a textbook. Our next class would be entirely taken up with checking to see if we had done our homework. The pupils would have to describe what they had read or recite passages from memory. This was, of course, tedious for the person who had to recite and for those who had to listen, not to mention the teacher. I remember I used to stand at the blackboard, struggling to remember just *what* had been written about Larina in chapter 5 or 6, or what the teacher had said about her. It would sometimes happen that the teacher would prompt us, but once again, no more than what was "scheduled" was allowed—only what the curriculum demanded.

I remember when our teacher made her own "personal" remarks about the heroine's behavior. Her remarks were not about the passage in which Tatyana agrees to be the faithful wife of the old man, but about the passage in which Larina writes her famous letter to Onegin. Our literature teacher looked sternly around the class, and said, "Tatyana wrote her letter to Onegin. It was her fortune that he turned out to be a proper young man. Because it certainly could have turned out much worse—she could have become a laughingstock, the object of vicious gossip. Things don't usually work out like that in real life. So I would advise our young girls not to be blind to her example." That was all that our teacher, a "builder of communism," had to say to us, the future "builders of communism." Maybe the poor thing had had bitter experiences in life herself, but her wise advice was impossible to take seriously. It all just sounded too insipid. And it had nothing to do with the poem itself—the poem to which we were supposed to be applying ourselves.

We studied Tolstoy's *War and Peace* in the same way. It all came down to our copying the basic ideas, images, and themes as dictated to us by our teacher. We did it mechanically, without stopping to reflect on anything. Basically, we copied down from dictation everything that we were supposed to know. The novel was broken down into several lessons. And then suddenly we had a free period—our teacher got sick. As usual, it was assumed that students should not be allowed to sit without supervision (even though we were allowed to do so outside, for some reason; apparently on the street we were not students anymore). A substitute teacher was sent in, and she ordered us to write a composition on any theme relating to the novel. What freedom! One of our classmates wrote that she simply did not like Lev Tolstoy because of his erroneous understanding of the role of women in society. We handed in our notebooks, and on the next day we got them back. But this student who said she disliked Tolstoy did not get hers back. Instead, she was summoned by our literature teacher, who was well by now and back on the job. The student was taken aside and scolded as if she had done something naughty and shameful. She was told that Tolstoy was a literary giant and she would never equal him. She had no moral right to criticize the great Tolstoy. The teacher gave her an assignment to write another essay, but this time on a new subject. This girl has kept her dislike for Tolstoy to this day.

This type of response to any attempt at independent thinking is widespread in the Soviet Union, and not only in schools. In truth, we remain pupils (scholars) for our entire lives. We are picked apart at meetings of the "collective" at factories, we are purged at student seminars, and in the end we are summoned to the KGB for a "chat," or ordered to report to the police because one of the neighbors in our communal apartment has informed on us.

All this begins in early childhood, in the elementary school. Everything goes back to that. But no matter how much the development of women's character is hindered, it will never be as easy to do as it used to be in earlier days when the female sex was in bondage.

Today the idea of freedom is wafting through the air, and the psyches of young girls are changing radically. The democratization of clothing plays an indirect role—when fashions are unisex, the borders between what is strictly male and what is strictly female are washed away. In the 1960s, people in the Soviet Union first became acquainted with many theories that had already been explored in the rest of the world during our "iron curtain" period. In the 1970s, the flood of theoretical information was stemmed somewhat, but by then an active, practical absorption of these ideas had already begun. In the 1960s, women who dared to wear pants were laughed at in the cities, and stones were thrown at them on the collective farms. In the 1970s, the "woman with the cowboy look" came into fashion. Girls began wearing jeans, and this became a symbol of emancipation for them. True, it was a kind of emancipation that was only valued in public. The family did not approve of this, nor did the school. Those punitive lessons in literature, taught by indifferent people (the most effective were those trained in the Stalin era), created sharp contrasts for us between our studies and real life. They created an atmosphere of mistrust and a (temporary) hypocritical acquiescence. School is like a check mark on a registration form. But where does this form go? To the future?

Translated by Catherine A. Fitzpatrick

About the New Americans

EKATERINA MIRONOVA
Moscow, Russia

Now, since the patriarchy is receding and will clearly sink into oblivion, women are breathing the fresh air of freedom, opening wide their lungs like wings and taking deep breaths. They look like prisoners who have just emerged from an underground where they have spent many long years. Women are hurrying to shed the clothing that was intended for men's erotic arousal. They are leaping onto horses and straddling them; they are running along the beach, pressing their bare feet into the moist sand.

The disregard for women's sexual needs, characteristic of the patriarchy (the majority of women never knew an orgasm to their dying days), was related to the "consumer attitude" toward the female body in general. They shoved it into corsets, bodices, tight shoes and skirts, all of which restricted movement and deprived the body of its natural freedom. Both the soul and body of women were transformed into the shape of a vessel that was pleasing to men, much as the Chinese did when they deliberately bred grotesque people for the amusement of the emperor.

All feminism, it seems to me, is a gratifying phenomenon, although some of its forms could become unacceptable in the future. This is a period of trial and error. Naturally in some cases "production costs" are unavoidable. Women's spontaneous protest against enslavement is occurring again and again in ever-widening circles, encompassing new aspects as it ripples outward. Even in earlier times there were outbreaks of resistance and revolts. And at the beginning of the century a movement was organized that, like any new phenomenon, was rich in both positive and negative elements. The neofeminism of our era shines bright and is already unstoppable, and it finds its most expansive expression in the United States. Emancipated American women often conform to the male stereotype, and I detect a similarity in this tendency with the Soviet emancipation; both U.S. and Soviet forms of emancipation apparently can be explained by the specific character of the superpowers. Some of our women try to join the patriarchal world that is alien to them by using coarse and vulgar language. And our women are rude not only in their speech but also in their manners; the clashes on buses, in stores, and in communal apartments are disgraceful and sometimes reach a point when both men and women resort to physical force. But the similarity between female emancipation in the two superpowers is not total. The United States is democratic in its structure and therefore its women's liberation movement is also much broader and more sharply focused. Women's banks, cafés, and libraries—we do not have such things yet and at the moment it is hard to imagine them. American cultural advancement and the powerful struggle for women could probably catch on here. Occasionally our young women take classes in karate, but the mass conservatism inhibits this. Certainly one can agree that women do not need such training, because it distorts their nature. But do we know enough about this organism called woman? Too many taboos connected with women have grown up over the course of the years.

Darwin has a very amusing supposition that the female of ancient times was bearded like the male, not to mention the fact that she conceded him nothing in physical strength. Again, cultural advancement is just the right to choose. In the final analysis, women will figure things out in this chaos of feminist tendencies. At present the society in which women must develop mountains of muscles to prove themselves seems ridiculous. But perhaps the biceps developed by American women sports enthusiasts just show the possibilities of the female organism, possibilities that were heretofore unknown to civilization. People rely heavily on hereditary signs to distinguish one person from another, irrespective of sex. Some are drawn to sports, with its speed and fresh air, while others prefer the library with its books.

If we are talking about women's political and sexual independence, then something should be said about physical freedom. This freedom has already found expression in comfortable T-shirts made of natural materials, in light and practical tennis shoes, in roller skates, and in morning runs, recommended for everyone. It seems to me that sports benefit women and will help them free themselves once and for all. Of course, a sport is perverted when, having become a profession, it limits a person, narrowing his or her horizons and possibilities for full realization. The drugs and hormonal preparations used in professional sports to increase women's performance are undoubtedly hazardous to their health and represent the antithesis of the goals of physical education. In any given instance, drugs and hormonal preparations can have irreversible effects on the female body, disfigure her, and disturb her psyche. Sports are symbolized by the freedom of the body and the joy of motion. Modern gymnasts and figure skaters charm us no less than the young women of Sparta who competed in contests with young men, unashamed of their nakedness. The Greek runner, carved by an ancient sculptor, is like our contemporary women who boldly conquer the height of the parallel bars or the narrowness of the balance beam. But these kinds of sports are particularly suited to women, are like second nature to them.

Let us return to the American enthusiasts. It is no secret that women are muscular by nature. More often than not their muscles are a burden to them and they try to hide them from people's sight. Here the same old patriarchal (or more precisely sexist) corset plays a role. Among men, both the *bogatyr*[1] and the "elf" (the poet, dancer, midget) are romanticized. But a woman must not be anything but an "elf." And what if she is a female *bogatyr*, with a hereditary athletic build? In ancient Rus' there used to be a specific concept of a *polenitsa* (a female *bogatyr*). Such women were not simply Amazons like those we see in the Hermitage Museum. They were large women (as history tells us), muscular, hardy, and used to riding steeds as heavy as they were. The Russian *polenitsa* in folk epic poetry reflects clear traces of a matriarchy among the Slavs. Modern women should also be unashamed of their physical strength if they are physically strong by nature, and feel free to develop their strength if they want to do so. After all, physically powerful women are not necessarily mannish. They can be beautiful in their strength and might. Is it not precisely the might of Ella Fitzgerald's voice that bewitches us? And Edith Piaf, little Edith Piaf—what low notes she attains imitating "the old days of Lucien!" Perhaps the extreme tendencies of international feminism will lead not to an identification with the male world but rather to an awareness of the variety of human nature that is now also female. In one of Mikhail Sholokhov's Cossack tales there is a description of a physical struggle in a village between a man and a woman. The woman did not concede to the man and that aroused a sense of admiration among the spectators. The female sex has always had its *bogatyrs* who bashfully kept silent. Here there are very fine gradations. Incidentally, the widespread formula "men and women fought side by side" is insincere because women are supposedly being flattered by being made equal to men and are simultaneously being "raised" to their level. This level has been created by the protracted trampling of women and at their expense.

1. A hero in Russian folklore, roughly comparable to Hercules.

Therefore there is no need to raise them to that level. They will raise themselves by their own strength somehow. The falseness of that formula lies in the fact that we never hear the corresponding formula "men and women cleaned (did the laundry, washed the floor or the windows) side by side." Of course not! That would be humiliating for the men.

When I hear that a particular country is introducing military service for women, I make a correction (or rather a clarification) to myself: "Yes, but the service is voluntary, not obligatory, for women are part of the service of the human race. They are the mothers of human beings. And when they realize that fully, there will be an end to wars." But not all ships are military ships and teen-agers of both sexes dream of becoming sea cadets or even captains. Why is it that when they are coming of age, young men have the opportunity to realize their dreams but young women do not? The insignificant number of young women who get the opportunity to work on a ship do so as cleaners or cooks. Their position on board a ship is far from what they dreamed of. There is something third-class about it in the general view. Unlike their male counterparts, young women cannot enter the two-year maritime courses and sail abroad as full-fledged members of the crew. It is unusual to find women doctors aboard a ship. For the most part they are forced out of that position by male doctors, and not because the men are better qualified. No, it is simply that the men prefer the sea to a stuffy clinic, where the women doctors race like squirrels on their drums in a cage.

I would guess there are two or three women with the rank of captain, but this must be viewed as a remnant of the war period. In most instances, a woman must possess extraordinary capabilities to overcome the unbelievable obstacles in her path, as did, for example, Larisa Reissner, a commissar of the Revolution. During the war many of our women took active part, and not just as nurses. They were snipers, reconnaissance officers, and pilots. Generations of women remember this—grandmothers, mothers, daughters, and granddaughters. Little girls see old military photographs in the family album, hear stories, and it is only natural that some of them develop a desire to go into the army. But adolescence is sensitive to romance, although the experience often turns out later to be pseudoromance, and girls must come to understand this on their own. They need experience, but instead they are put in their places and forbidden to pursue their convictions. The stifling atmosphere of everyday life that hangs over them maims them more than the sea or the artillery range could. In the 1960s there was a brief liberal craze and some of my women friends went off to studios and studied fencing, karate, pantomime, and rowing. They got a lift and a sense of joy from their activities but everyone soon abandoned them for one reason or another, all except one woman who became a professional athlete. Therefore, when masses of young American women proclaim, "We don't want to be just sexual objects for men anymore!" or young Japanese women go to the police to master the arts of karate and jujitsu, I am on their side. Maybe they will not become "geniuses of judo," but are athletic results our only goal?

They say that love and hunger rule the world. But if I can say "I live for love," then I cannot say "I live to eat." Wine and cigarettes give us sensations that are close to love. Theatrical attractions, swings, and carousels stir up a dizziness in us characteristic of love. Sports, like dance, imitate love, varying our physical possibilities. Love is life itself. And everything that approaches love enriches our lives and frees our vital energy—so sings the hymn of life.

Translated by Rebecca Park

Between Women

Visitors to the Soviet Union often notice the open physical affection between people of the same sex. It is common to see women holding hands, walking arm in arm, embracing and kissing. Close friendships between women are the norm; given the lack of mobility in Soviet life, these ties may extend from grade school to old age. As recent films (*Moscow Does Not Believe in Tears* is a good example) indicate, female friends provide support through crises in relationships with men and in some cases remain closer and more trusted than spouses.

Such closeness does not necessarily indicate that lesbianism is accepted or widespread. Soviets, like most people outside the U.S., are more physically demonstrative; they do not equate touching with sexuality. Taboos against homosexuality remain strong; they have been reinforced by Soviet laws and puritanism.

This has not always been the case. The Soviet Union was the first state to abolish all laws against homosexuality. In 1934, however, Stalin personally encouraged a law making male homosexuality a crime punishable by imprisonment of up to eight years. Although lesbianism is not illegal, gay women can be confined in mental hospitals and are subject to loss of job, designation as an unfit mother, and other harassment.

Mistress of the High Mountain

LYUBOV RAZUMOVSKAYA
Magnitogorsk, Urals, Russia

I first saw her in a television movie based on Bazhov's fables.
She was a very convincing and authentic Mistress of the Copper Mountain. Indeed, it was in my native Urals that this
image was born, the image of the beautiful stone woman capable of turning into an emerald-green lizard or a vein of mala-
chite or a cornflower—a speck of azure in the thick of the
mountain. This mysterious ruler of the Ural Mountains was
able to be ruthless with the greedy and wicked, and tender
with the hard-working and kind. I had known this story since
childhood; it is the first fairy tale that I remember. But I had
never imagined her so alive, so real. Alisa Freindlikh was her
name—that was what I learned from the credits on the television show. I also learned that my Mistress of the Copper
Mountain did not live in our Urals, but in a distant, large
northern city, and that she was a famous actress. I could not
get rid of the vision of her face, her figure, her voice. I just
had to see her in person. But I was a mere fifteen years old.
There was school. Parents.

I almost stopped looking at my schoolbooks. I searched for
books about her in all the bookstores and libraries, and any
journals or articles about this Alisa Freindlikh, with her photograph. Finally I got on a train and hid myself in an upper
berth, and by almost a miracle I made it to Moscow. I had
some bread crusts and a ticket, according to which I was supposed to get out long before the capital. When I tried to get
on the train to Leningrad, I was detained (I was not able to
show any ID) and handed over to the police. In the police sta-

tion I sat with a drunk and a little twelve-year-old boy who had run away from home. Soon I was taken back to Magnitogorsk. When I was asked why I had done this, I answered, "Love led me."

Somehow I managed to finish high school (the school year was just coming to an end) and I arranged to go to Leningrad. I signed up for a construction project and was given a registered place in a dormitory—what we call a limit, which means you can only stay there and in Leningrad as long as you keep the job. The work was heavy and dirty and I often grew exhausted and homesick. But in compensation, I went to the LenSoviet Theater every night, where Alisa Freindlikh was playing. I saw all the plays in which she had roles many times over, and I saw her leave the theater. In the foyer and behind stage there were always crowds of ecstatic boys and girls (the kind of young people who are always hangers-on at theaters— talented people and admirers. I did not join them and felt lonely). I would only go to the theater with my dormitory roommate, a slender, tiny girl, almost an adolescent. She worked as a nurse in a home for the aged.

I couldn't make up my mind to approach Alisa after the show, and many times I followed her silhouette disappearing into the city fog or behind a veil of rain. She never noticed me. Her fans met her at the exit, wearing blue jeans, slick and self-assured. I felt so insignificant. Once my girlfriend and I went to the theater. I bought a bouquet of roses and asked her to take them to Alisa. That was how our acquaintance began.

When people ask me how she is dressed, how she carries herself, how she speaks, I do not know what to say. "What do you mean?" they ask, incredulous. "You were right next to her; you must have talked about something." I cannot say anything and just smile in embarrassment. I see her eyes before me, the smile that penetrates to the heart. I hear her words in my ears, "Thank you, dear!" She did not even call me by name;

she just said it simply, and I felt like pressing myself to her, or at least touching her. She shook my hand and even now I feel the touch of her fingers.

It seems that in just another moment happiness will be in your hands. But right at that moment a taxi pulls up and takes her far, far away. And once again, you race after it, seizing a moment of fortune. Does a person need much? No, not much at all, a second and an eternity. Just a glance—but let it be eye to eye. Just a word, but a word meant for him or her and not thin air. Just a breath, but a breath of tenderness.

Passionate desire would appeal to her: "Either with tenderness or harshness, either with a caress or with shyness, either with vows or with silence, either with joy or desire."

Happiness? Today, I am the happiest person in the world—tomorrow, the most sorrowful. A person always lacks something for lasting happiness. After the play *Dulcinea Tobosskaya*, I asked her, "Excuse me, are you happy?" I gave her a question that has an answer, but she just plaintively sang, "Let me be happy, forget about everything and sing songs." It seemed to me that she must have been in great pain when she hurled out these words to the audience, too loud, too bitter: "Every woman wants to be Dulcinea—even for an hour, even for a second, even in her sleep, even in her dreams." At times she did not so much sing as shout out the words, which embarrassed and worried me. In *Warsaw Melody* she sang in Polish and spoke with a charming accent that made her seem like a little child; the mood was entirely different, but there was sadness there, too.

They say that Leningrad and the rain are inseparable. Even now it is sleeting all the harder on the rapidly emptying streets. The rain briskly chases away passers-by, carefully washes the old roofs of the houses, and then for a long time admires itself, so gray and long. It probably thinks it wonderful to see itself reflected in the polish of the roofs it has washed. That must be why it cleans everything around it so carefully, washing every window, every leaf of every tree, every statue, trying to destroy the dust caked on everything and wash it away, washing away everything until at last it sees its own reflection.

I walk home soaked to the skin even with an umbrella in hand. But the umbrella only rescues my head; the rain ruthlessly pours down the rest of my body. I shiver from the cold, from the wind off the Neva River that penetrates to my very bones. My clothes become rough and stick to my skin. My clothes cannot save me, but it seems as if they try to seek warmth and shelter from the warmth of my body. Even so, I love the rain, perhaps because it is so inseparable from this city. I often wander along the slippery streets under its torrent. When there is no rain for a long time, I begin to suffocate from the city dust that accumulates everywhere. The rain also chokes from the dust. That is why it comes with a gray and somber face. Even I cringe when I see its fierce countenance. It is angry that so much dust has gathered in its absence, dust that no one else wants anything to do with except the native Leningrader. In silence, I walk beside it, afraid to be the first to start a conversation and provoke its displeasure with a careless remark. We turn from Rubinstein Street into a small lane and I see a lonely female figure walking with a quick step. She is so fragile and helpless that I involuntarily draw near her and offer her my umbrella. When the rain is so ruthless, formalities are silly and strangers crouch under the same cover, even under such an inadequate one as my umbrella. I hold up this thin cloth on its slender spokes, which barely withstand the gusts of wind; I hold it up over the head of a woman. She turns, her lips whisper thanks.

Oh, God! I step back. I see before me the dear face, the beloved face, of Alisa, the face that is like no other, the face of Alisa Freindlikh. I squeeze my eyes shut—is it a delusion? I

open them—no, it is really she! I look at her with fright and
rapture. I am seized by feverishness—I can be useful to her,
needed now, here, in this passageway with my pathetic umbrella. She catches my hand and squeezes it in a friendly way.
I tremble from her touch. My heart is beating treacherously
loud. I furtively press my hand to my chest so that she does
not hear its beating, that loud beating of my heart, drowning
out the noise of the rain. We are completely alone; there are
no passers-by in sight. I so much want my friends to see me
walking with this woman, next to her, along the street, to the
roar of the rain, to the music of her voice. Streams of water
flood down me, preventing me from seeing her. Now and then
I wipe these streams from my face, but my hand is completely
wet and it is pointless. Alisa, seeing my unsuccessful struggle
with the rain and my wet, guilty smile, takes out a handkerchief from her pocket. We stop and she tries to dry my face.
Her hand touches my lips, the bridge of my nose, my cheeks,
my chin, and I am really awake; it is not in a dream that I
feel her warm, shaky breath. I obediently turn my face to meet
the movements of her hand. I squint as from the sun's rays
and pray to myself, "Oh, time, stand still! Freeze this moment,
hold her hand on my face, hold those sun rays of her fingers."
I thought of nothing but this. Her small, warm palm tries to
accomplish something, but the rain is pouring buckets and the
streams of water flow down my face once again. Alisa suddenly
starts to laugh silently. I open my eyes and see how she is looking at me gaily, the end of her tongue protruding a little. She
carefully wrings out her handkerchief, which managed to soak
up so much water from my face that using it now is practically impossible. The archness of her expression, the mischie-
vous, sharp tip of her tongue, her helpless hands holding the
wet hanky—all this made me laugh. She laughs, too. The rain
continues to play on its clavichord, and our laughter rings out
in dissonance with it. The rain attacks us again and begins to

drum on my poor umbrella so hard that it seems about to break through it. We laugh all the louder. The rain envelops us with a live spider's web, blocking out the light. We keep tripping over obstacles in the dark, landing in puddles and splashing our legs with stinging cold water. It is both terrible for us and funny. Alisa stops periodically, first lifting up her right leg, then her left, taking off her shoes one by one and letting out a long "Aaaah." She pours out the water from these tiny boats fallen prey to the elements. She leans on me with one arm and wrinkles her face in desperation, putting on her leather shoes now soaked through with water.

Finally we reach our destination. At the entrance, Alisa holds out her hand and shakes my hand firmly and warmly. "My little wet sparrow," she says, her hand caressing my hair, which is all stuck together. Lowering my eyes to control my overwhelming feelings, I duck my head and Alisa suddenly embraces me. Pressing myself to her, I feel like a child, and large, joyful tears course down my cheeks and mix with the rain. Alisa does not see my tears, and I do not want her to see them. Alisa winks at me playfully and disappears into a half-dark entryway.

And I run. I splash through the puddles, spraying water in all directions, splashing the glass of the telephone booths and the posters hung too low. I spill out my joy, my happiness, to the houses, to the occasional oncoming cars, to the even rarer passers-by. I run, and behind me are the wings of the rain.

> If I could have your rights
> Be like you and in that succeed
> But then, who will take my place before you,
> And who will dare sing these songs of praise?
>
> Bella Akhmadulina

She passes by this time with a quick step, looking down at her feet and not noticing me. Every movement of her body said that she wanted to be alone now with her thoughts. She walked along as if she wanted to dissolve into that gloomy Leningrad day, to get home without anyone noticing her. I follow her with my eyes, entirely transfixed by her being—not trying to catch up with her and talk to her. I was overflowing with just the fact of seeing her, so aloof, retreating into herself. With every nerve, with every cell, I sensed how close she was to me. I love her entirely, with all her good traits and shortcomings, with all that is peculiar only to her, without which she would not be Alisa Freindlikh. I love her with all the good and bad qualities of her heroines: "in no way attractive," "horribly shy," "overanxious," "coarse," "tactless," always so different, never repeating anything. She is always new; she always finds something new in herself and cultivates it every day. But it was essential for her to be new. For herself. For us, her viewers. On the stage she would literally perform miracles of giving: She would merge with her heroine to such an extent that the play ceased to be a play. Before us was a new, live person. Sometimes suddenly and unexpectedly. Here she is, a travesty, playing not a woman but a boy; she who was already forty, with a daughter, played a small boy in the play *The Little Boy and Karlson Who Lived on the Roof*. So much fervor and pathos in the image that Alisa Freindlikh created—one could believe she was the little boy. And her slightly incorrect bite (a defect that the Theatrical Institute Commission treats severely) only lent her a special charm, emphasizing her individuality. Or let us take *The Fifth Decade,* a script written especially for her about a simple woman entering the fifth decade of her life, a little sad and very true to life, like everything else about Alisa.

My mother died. It always seemed to me that she did not

understand me, but now that she is gone I feel very guilty toward her. The darkness of her death, the emptiness in her place—all that suddenly made me grow up. And that weight of adulthood fell on me, settled on my shoulders, not with wings but as a burden. Even so, something inside me improved significantly. How small my native town seemed to me after Leningrad. As if I had outgrown it. But the Urals, the Urals remain big, expansive, just as rich with semiprecious stones as before. So remains my Mistress of the Copper Mountain, her bright light shining there in the distance—I had carried it away with me.

When I learned of my mother's death, I could not work, and asked for time off. I was not granted this; there was an overload at work, and I was only allowed three days for the funeral. Then I quit my job and went back to Magnitogorsk. Naturally, I lost my registration at the dormitory (it goes with the job), and I do not see any way of going back. In my room, next to the portrait of my mother, hangs a portrait of Alisa Freindlikh, a portrait from fifteen years ago. I had hung it there long before I even left for Leningrad.

Translated by Catherine A. Fitzpatrick

The Right to Be Myself

INESSA TOMINAITE
Vilnius, Lithuania

*And in the Soviet Union we are nonconformists. Even
in our progressive Baltic states, to which people from all
parts of our country flock as to a miniature version of the
West, the same methods of repression are used against
lesbians as against dissidents.*

"But you're a girl!" I was teased.

"You should still be reading *The Young Guard*,[1] I was told
at twenty when I selected Nietzsche.

And I just wanted to be a person, to read independently
from the wishes of the librarian, and not to be limited in my
affections by sexual stereotypes.

But as far as that went, no one had any criticism against
me. It was even the opposite—my purely friendly relations
with boys provoked many reproaches and accusations. Oh,
they were all so vigilant on that score!

I was an emotional and sensitive adolescent. But at an early
age, the system of school discipline killed in me the necessity
of outwardly showing these feelings. Thus in my character
evaluations the words "quiet" and "even-tempered" appeared.
The need never arose to share with anyone at all the intimate
details of my life.

Girls started to fall in love with me at age ten or twelve.
Head over heels. I do not know why. Perhaps they sensed some

1. *The Young Guard* (*Molodaia Gvardia*) is a Soviet literary journal for
young people.

sort of inner strength in me. Or took my yearning for independence as such a strength. It was adoration. Worship. With jealousy, tears. And without excluding erotic motives. And later, with regret about my sexual orientation. I was carefully protected from boys, but I played erotic games with girls.

I very often fell in love. The constancy of this feeling was for me just as natural and necessary as was my sense of hearing for a fuller knowledge of the world. And it was my world. Along with books, which they stubbornly refused to give me. And I wanted to find myself in them. Not to identify myself with a man! I had already become aware of my "abnormality." Or you could say, I became aware of what was normal *for me*. Books were silent on the subject, and instead, with scornfully curled lips, authors angrily slung mud. If even in typical relations the man and woman are inevitably harnessed to the bed, then in my situation the bed becomes a skyscraper into which women (filthy, of course!) crowd in a sexual fever. Imagine with what ugly associations the word *lesbian* appeared to me.

I could not relate to men even though I tried. I knew and sensed them too well. The conniving, constant sacrificing of one's self was humiliating for me. I sensed myself to be above that and stronger. A man could not be my ideal. I could not sense my own unworthiness next to him. Is it possible to bow down from above? From my height, I saw women who were cruelly unnoticed by men. I could not bow down to them. For me, the physical connection was far from necessary. I valued in those women what men stubbornly refused to see.

The first time I seriously fell in love (when I say "seriously" I mean strongly and fully), it was with a woman who was older than I. We took more than a year to come together. Running parallel, and at the same time in different directions. At that time I abruptly severed my relations with everyone else. We met only when we turned out to be free from all barriers. But by then it was too late. I could no longer gather and hold the drops of love. Everything was squeezed out. I had already mentally lived through everything, and even then, everything was coming to a climax.

Without a doubt, she liked me. Otherwise she would not have started to cross the barrier between the teacher and student. We were forced to break up. At first she made a trip to Moscow, then she remained there.

I was left completely alone. Among unknown people. Without any opportunity to return to anyone. All around me people talked about husbands and lovers—men. There was no one with whom I could even breathe a word about my trouble. But the funniest thing was that everyone sought my advice. Inwardly I was groaning, but I could do nothing. If suddenly in a conversation my painful problem was brought up, it was only with a half-scornful laugh (by people who were "in the know"—the kind of people who, when listening to Tchaikovsky, for example, do not smile because of their pleasure with the music, but because they know about him).

Right at that time I ran across Veresayev's essay "Sappho," in which he attempts to whitewash the poetess. He is condescending in his attitude toward male love, indignant at the thought of female love ("filthy and unnatural"). True, he cites Plato's *Symposium* on the predominance of the "how" over the "what." The quote in that text is entirely accidental; it is the view of a man negating the possibility of a woman's enjoyment without his participation.

Thus two years passed. And still I was lucky. L. appeared at our institute. Now there were two of us. We did not see in each other that universal, obvious hostility, and that helped us to open up to each other. Did we love each other? I do not know. At any rate, our five-year friendship, to the surprise and amazement of those around us, was without fights or scandals, and so it was our property. L. was a difficult person. Egocentric. Capricious. I also had these shortcomings, so our relation reached a balance—and most importantly, equality. We came to the conclusion that we had to look for our kind in the theater crowd. We began to listen to "those in the know" and finally selected one name. Flowers? The stage door? Anything but that! But what? I dialed a number and simply told the woman who answered that I loved her. Evidently I sounded sincere. The words, awaited for so long, tapping feelings hidden deep underground, were too convincing. Soon we met and I was granted the chance to *love*. And I really did fall in love. Although the words of love had been uttered too early, they turned out to be pathetic, impoverished creatures in comparison with the discovered feeling. True, this did not interfere with my being involved in the most tender relations with L. But I made a mistake. I should never have allowed myself to concentrate everything so completely on one person. The breakup occurred because of a silly phone call from L. that unsettled me for a long time. It was pure curiosity! L. asked the actress what relations we had. And that was with a universal fear of publicity! There do exist, of course, those who are "unmasked." They openly dress as boys. They even flaunt their orientation. Basically, those were part of the so-called nonworking. It was impossible to create some "public opinion" around them because there was no need for them to hide anything.

The state of shock did not pass for a long time. But when I temporarily came to, I threw myself into a whirl of debauchery. If a woman carelessly showed me any sympathy, without making a spectacle I managed to get her to fall in love with me, and then I would disappear. I was furious that people only saw the boy in me. How many "compliments" did I hear about my masculinity, male character, male self-assurance, and male fickleness!

In crossing the border of generally accepted relations, these women projected themselves into newly formed relations. Is it worth it to cross that line? But these women do not have any example to follow for new forms of relating. And how can they be created, with such dissociation and the impossibility at this stage for us to unite? I have met people who continue relations that have long outlived themselves only because of the fear of remaining alone. And then it is so much harder for us to find our other half. On this problem we should look at the *Symposium* once again, at the myth about the people who were punished for their pride and were doomed to search for their other half. Not only two-sexed creatures were among them. Why are man and woman in such a cage? Why should I go against my nature? The health of society is obtained not by force. Forcing it can only cause nervous discomfort. There are already enough reasons for stressful situations in our lives. The intimate life is still the only territory where an individual can reign. Why deprive us of that last private domain? For me, what has become the norm for others is unnatural. I am speaking only of the right to be myself, to not have to submit to the punishment of a people who have an unacceptable culture.

And in the Soviet Union, we are dissidents—"those who think otherwise." Even in our progressive Baltic republics, where people come from all ends of the Soviet Union as others go to the West, the same methods of suppression used against dissidents are used against lesbians.

Translated by Catherine A. Fitzpatrick

Verses from the Cycle
"To My Contemporary"

YELENA LASTENKO
Anapa, Crimea

You say, "Madness and childhood." [1]
I feel cold and you say, "Get dressed."
Get dressed? That will not help me.
What advice can one give to a wave?
What advice can one give to a wall?
You will go away and you probably will not remember
    me.
You will be thinking far and wide,
And the thoughts will be: "time period," "answer,"
    "reproach,"
And the thoughts will be of another spring,
About anything at all, but not about me.

From morning till night—the nymph and concubine,
The flower, and the prostitute, and the poet.
And claws of pain, sharp like scissors,
Are sticking into me and the light is going out.
The sun appears, then hides,
The wind blows, then it abates again.
Your concubine, your storyteller!
But how can I tell you the story of my love?
How can I express it? I do not want to color it.
I would do better to simply turn toward the wal .
But you go right ahead, do not trust me, quest on me,

---

1. In the Russian text it is clear through certain grammatical constructions that both the speaker and the person addressed are women.

151

So that all the strings in me snap,
So that if I fall asleep I will dream something terrify-
    ing,
So that in the morning I will not open my eyes.
I am strong, I am evil, I am fearless.
God forbid that I should finish my story.
The phases, the days, and the stories are numbered.
How slowly the leaf circles over the asphalt.
How it circles, how it circles.
Does it comfort you? It is so hard to find
The words that will comfort you.
Shall I say that there will be other holidays—
Other eyes and other people more simple,
Others who are better, and perhaps others who are
    worse?
Houses and sunsets, enemies and poets,
But not what we had, not that, no, not that.

And the wind is forcing the window—
You are not dressed for the weather.
And someone black enters quietly:
"That's it, your time has run out."
And I rush, as in a dream,
To the pen, to the last salvation.
No one waits till Sunday[2]
So that the wounds on me have healed.
No one waits for me in the darkness
To comfort me or simply
To take me to the country churchyard.[3]

---

2. The Russian word for Sunday is identical to the word for resurrection
except for one slight variation in spelling. Undoubtedly the author has
chosen the word with the double meaning in mind.
3. The word for country churchyard in Russian is *pogost*, which has a
second, more elaborate meaning of "country church together with ceme-
tery and clergy house and adjacent buildings."

Am I in my right mind—
Whence the pain, whence the shivering?
After all, I am dressed for the weather.
But someone black enters quietly:
"Leave her and don't disturb her."
And I then will be alone on the street,
And you then will be alone in your train compartment.
How shameful to cry and stoop,
And to be stingy with myself.
But this night, so black it is
In the capricious scattering of lights!
Oh, had I, learned in everything,
Only been able to lose myself in it.
Oh, had I, such a proud woman,
Only forgotten suddenly that I am proud
And had just gone for a walk about town
And never returned.
And let us be acquitted for all this.
I will not be able to understand and I will not be able
     to bear
How I then will be alone on the street,
And you then will be alone in your train compartment.

I am mute, empty—
It is unlikely that we are going the same way.
I am not the one, not simple,
And for that, forgive me.
For the verse crudely thrown together,
Written with a chill up and down my spine.
I love you. What is to be done,
Forgive me for that too.

                    Translated by Rebecca Park

"With the grandeur of Homer and the purity of Sappho . . ."

ZHANNA IVINA
Tallinn, Estonia

For the title of my essay I have taken John Updike's words, with which he described Vladimir Nabokov's novel *Ada*. I am not going to attempt to write about *Ada*—Updike has already done that. I merely want to draw the reader's attention to the distinctiveness and undoubted precision of the attribute "sapphic purity." It is sufficient unto itself, whatever might be added on to it—it is an indestructible phrase. Set side by side, these two words not only do not contradict each other, but rather one reinforces the other. Having dared to touch on this theme, I have intentionally chosen two poets who are stylistically very different. But surely a difference in style or period does not hinder a spiritual affinity. I have chosen true poets, for whom it is unimportant to which nation they belong, or to which sex, or to which century. And so, we have Marina Tsvetaeva, a woman, a Russian woman of the twentieth century, and Walt Whitman, a man, a nineteenth-century American. Both are brilliant articulators of a cosmic consciousness, of the intuitive thought of poetic foresight. Without violence these poets tear up (blow up!) the accustomed boundaries of early existence. And if they are unable to liberate other people from invisible chains, that is not their fault. In order to free oneself, the other person must also become a poet. Then, intoxicated with life, that person pulsates on meeting it:

Passing stranger! you do not know
how ardently, how longingly I look
upon you.
You must be he I was seeking everywhere
somewhere
I ate with you and slept with you
Your body has become not yours only
nor left my body mine only . . .

That's Walt Whitman. This is Marina Tsvetaeva:

You pass along on your way
And I don't even touch your hand.
but there is an anguish inside of me—
it is so endless,
would that you were to me like anyone else.

Straight away my heart cried out "beloved,"
For you it was just something passing
but I've said farewell now,
Knowing nothing, not even your name!
O, love me, just love me! . . .

The soul has no gender; this is the fundamental starting
point of a true poet. In the West, currently, they use the enig-
matic symbol "bi" (bisexual). Shame is hidden behind the
brevity and reserve of this symbol. But this concept (of bisexu-
ality) was absolutely indisputable for the American bard.

To walk for a time amongst the people,
To touch their bodies
To embrace now male, now female flesh
with my hands,
what more could I want . . .

In quite a different voice, but about that theme, Marina speaks:

> There are names like sultry blossoms,
> And looks there are, like a flame . . .
> There are dark, sinuous mouths
> With deep, moist corners.
>
> There are women with hair like helmets,
> Whose fans waft fatally, delicately,
> Perhaps they are thirty years of age,
> Why are you one of them?
> Why is mine the soul of a Spartan child?

Let me repeat that my task is not a comparison of Marina Tsvetaeva and Walt Whitman. But let there be for you, as there was for me, the joyful discovery of the unified nature of poetry, of the world of a poet. The poet allows the outside world to enter him, as it is; she opens herself out to the universe. There are no barriers for the poet, no restrictions.

> Women! why are you ashamed:
> You are the gateway of the body
> Even more, you are the gateway to the soul
> A woman is like the seed,
> The child is born unto a woman
> The man is born unto the woman.

For a poet the body is sacred: "If my body is not the soul, what then is my soul?" One can determine a poet by the unerring precision:

> I love you!—it's like a
>   thundercloud,

Like a sin above you!
Because you're biting and burning hot
And better than all the rest.

I love you because you and I are
    different,
Our lives diverge in the darkness
    of the byways,
And for your inspired temptations
    and your dark fate . . .

I love you for this trembling,
Because surely I must be dreaming?
And for this lovely irony
That you're you—and not him.

Poets solve the riddle of "sexual enigma." Through love they
have freed themselves from all kinds of fetters. Native moments
are a catharsis for them—a cleansing, a fiery illumination of
life's turmoil. Whether the poet turns to a "crucified woman"
or to a friend, his integrity is unblemished:

This is a female body,
And I am like a helpless mist
    over it.
And then everything falls away from me,
Everything disappears.

You are silent,
You for whom I wandered
    everywhere, often,
Only so that I could be near you . . .
But it didn't occur to you then,

> What a subtle, electric fire
>   burned in me,
> Because of you.

Poets foretell the future. Not for a minute do they forget that round about us are myriad worlds, behind us myriad centuries. They understand that the mankind of the future will need a tradition of democratic friendship, for more and more, in the hearts of people, there grows a new delicacy, a love of one's comrade, one's companion, of like-minded people. Whoever follows in the footsteps of the poet is torn from the lackluster mass of ordinary men and women.

> I remember with what sort of face
>   you entered,
> Without even the slightest blush,
> How you rose, biting your finger,
> Barely inclining your head.

> Your brow, with love for power
>   stamped on it
> Lies there
> Beneath the weight of a reddish
>   mask,
> Neither a woman nor a boy
> But something stronger than me.

> I rose with an unaccustomed movement,
> They had surrounded us,
> And in a joking tone someone said,
> "Let me introduce you, ladies and gentlemen!"

> And with a drawn-out movement you placed
>   your hand in mine,

On my palm there tenderly lingered
    A splinter of ice.

Already anticipating a clash,
With a sort of sideways glance
I half reclined in the chair,
Twisting the ring on my finger.

You took out a papirosi,
And I extended a match to you
Not knowing what I should do
Were you to look me
Straight in the face . . .

The charm of a different soul, a fascination with the very being, the essence of the spirit—this is the source of the poet's penchant for exalted friendships. This passionate attraction of the poet for another person, regardless of that person's sex, frightened Whitman's first commentators, accustomed as they were to the hypocritical reticence of their century and to its limitations. Not without alarm did they quote some of his more ardent lines from the cycle *Calamus*:

Whoever you are holding me now in hand,
Without one thing all will be useless,
I give you fair warning before you tempt me further,
I am not what you supposed, but far different.
Who is he that would become my follower?

The way is suspicious, the result uncertain, perhaps
    destructive,
You would have to give up all else, I alone would
    expect to be your sole and exclusive standard,

Your novitiate even then would be long and exhausting,
Therefore release me now before troubling yourself any
further, let go your hand from my shoulders,
Put me down and depart on your way.

Or else by stealth in some wood for trial,
Or back of a rock in the open air,
But just possibly with you on a high hill, first watching
lest any person for miles around approach unawares,
Or possibly with you sailing at sea, or on the beach of
the sea or some quiet island,
Here to put your lips upon mine I permit you,
With the comrade's long-dwelling kiss or the new hus-
band's kiss,
For I am the new husband and I am the comrade.
Or if you will, thrusting me beneath your clothing,
Where I may feel the throbs of your heart or rest upon
your hip . . .

Nowadays, when in the United States and Europe they talk
so much about "gay liberation," Marina Tsvetaeva's cycle of
verses *The Woman Friend* is not treated so severely:

I see your lips are sinuous
They reinforce your haughtiness,
And the way your rather severe brow protrudes
Grips my heart—takes it by storm!

Your dress is like a black silk coat of mail,
Your voice has the slightest touch of huskiness,
like a gypsy's,

Everything about you drives me to distraction,
Even the fact that you're not beautiful! . . .

You act the fool, be it with your fan, or with
   your walking stick,
In every fiber and every little bone,
In the shape of every naughty finger,
There's the delicacy of a woman, the impertinence
   of a boy.
I parry all your smiles with verse,
I open out the whole world to you
Everything is in store for us from you,
Unknown woman, with the brow of Beethoven!

This is not infamous "sex," it is the dynamics of sex, it is the equivalent movement of the soul. It is interesting that in their private lives both Whitman and Tsvetaeva were intentionally, exaggeratedly upright. The poet is simply calling things by their proper names, not veiling or defiling those things. And any object to which the poet turns blazes with triumphant brilliance:

Close, so closely above you
Do I whisper with my lips.
I have loved many men and women,
But none as I've loved you.

I beg you to excuse the number of quotes, but I wanted not so much to speak for the poets as to let them speak for themselves, the more so since our reading public barely has access to them.

Even on the eve of separation,
At love's ending,

I say again that I have loved these hands,
Your masterful hands.

And your eyes have I loved,
Demanding an account of any stray glance,
Not favoring someone—or anyone
With a look.

I love every bit of you,
You with that accursed passion—
God sees it!—
Demanding retribution
For any chance sigh . . .

Translated by the Women and Eastern Europe Group

Dropouts and Dissidents

Despite rigid residency and work rules and the requirement that everyone over sixteen have an internal passport, Soviet society has its dropouts. They may be the *bichi* (from *On the Beach*) or *bomzhi*, who live in vacant apartment buildings and expropriate their food from shops and stalls. Or they may be the drug addicts (some the children of highly placed officials) described by Ahmedova. They may be prostitutes or runaways, as are many of the young women in Soviet labor camps, or they may be more hardened criminals, part of a prison population rivaled in terms of percentage of the population only by the U.S. and South Africa.

Most dropouts are not overtly political, although at times the lines between dropouts and dissidents blur. This is especially true in the prisons and camps, where urban intellectuals, religious sectarians, and *bomzhi* may join forces in protesting unjust treatment. In more mundane circumstances, a dissident artist may become a dropout, dodging legal work to concentrate on her or his creative activity.

The dissident movement is diverse, including nationalists, religious sectarians, Jews, human rights advocates, workers fighting for free trade unions, democratic socialists and nonconformist artists, writers and poets. Little unites these groups beyond opposition to the Soviet government. The feminists fit under the dissident umbrella, although they are sharply critical of the sexist attitudes often found there.

A Day in the Life[1]

ZOYA GALITSKAYA
Donbas, Ukraine

I left my friends' house at 6:30 in the morning. It was May. In one of my jacket pockets I had a miniature alarm clock—a gift from my friends—and in the other pocket I had a single ruble. The day promised to be beautiful, so I decided to wander around town a little. In order not to make the crowds any worse, I set off on foot. Rush hour was approaching. People were racing to earn their daily bread, flying like birds, not even feeling the ground beneath their feet.

At the news kiosk, a line formed in a minute when they put out copies of *TV Guide*. Sensing that I was disrupting the harmony of the workday by looking like I was on a holiday, I stood at the end of the line and put on a deliberately businesslike expression. Two women, apparently girlfriends, were standing in line ahead of me and chatting back and forth.

"Nina, do you know what happened to Olga, Nastya's daughter?" asked the first woman, turning toward the second.

"No," said the second. "I haven't seen them for a long time —it's going on two years now."

"Oh, then listen to this!"

The storyteller's expression, which was harsh, somewhat arrogant, and self-satisfied, became unusually solemn and conspiratorial. Her whole manner spoke of the hardening of the Stalin years. She glanced over her shoulder, lowered her voice to a half-whisper, and began her story.

"Can you imagine, that little snotty-nosed brat, that sorry

1. The literal translation of the title of this story is "The Events of One Day."

169

little tenth grader got herself mixed up with a boy. He goes to the same high school as she does, but he's a year older, he's graduating now. Sure, he's handsome and talented, there's no question about it. So anyway, they were going out together, you know, meeting every day. And there was this drunk—his wife used to kick him out of the house every so often. So somehow this drunk showed them a cellar where he had gone through some hard times himself. He says to himself, Why should those kids be stuck out in the rain? Let them go in there and dry themselves off, he says, warm up a little, do a little smooching. Somewhere away from people's watchful eyes and idle tongues. What a sympathizer they found, the poor bastard. Well, they went and committed a sin in that cellar, and they didn't stop in time, they kept sinning almost every day. Of course, it wasn't long before Olga got herself pregnant. But she didn't breathe a *word* about it to a *soul*, not even her mother. She didn't even know herself, not for the longest time. She wasn't even aware that she was carrying a child until the baby started moving around inside her."

I recalled my own, similar story from some time ago. I became uncomfortable, and wanted to leave the kiosk, but curiosity got the upper hand and I stayed on to hear the story.

Out of tact, or perhaps for some other reason, the second woman, who had a kinder face, did not interrupt her girlfriend. She just raised her eyebrows from time to time and said, "Hmm . . ."

"At the high school, nobody had any suspicions either, not even her gym teacher. Then Nastya went away to the countryside for the summer. She wanted her daughter to come along with her, but Olga refused to go. She led her mother around by the nose, and then begged off, saying that she was going to visit a girlfriend. Hah! Some girlfriend! Then she moved right into that cellar so she could have fun with her sweetheart every night. I don't know why she didn't have a premature baby, carrying on like that. The two of them fixed up that cellar real fancy, so they could make themselves a little love nest. Those wanton little creatures!"

The line inched forward. The two women each bought *TV Guide.* I bought one, too, thinking it might come in handy later on. Then I dogged those two girlfriends in the hopes of finding out the end of the story. The women headed toward the metro without noticing me at all. The storyteller was gearing herself up for the climax.

"So Olga had her baby right there in that cellar, without any OB. She gave birth to a baby boy. He was a real cute little boy —had blonde hair, very healthy. Her boyfriend helped her give birth—see, he had started med school that year. Every day he would bring some food and clean diapers to the cellar from home. He'd wrap up the dirty ones and put them in his briefcase. Then when his parents were away, he'd wash, dry, and iron them. He also brought her cotton to use, and a space heater, and baby bottles—anything and everything that little baby needed. When they wanted to give the baby a bath, they'd draw water from the pipes in the basement. They used a big cardboard box for a cradle. Olga would take the baby out for an airing only at night. So that was how they got on.

"When the first of September rolled around, Olga was supposed to start school, you see; she was supposed to go into the tenth grade. That was when everyone suddenly wised up. First the teachers noticed her absence. Then Nastya came back from summering in the country. She got worried and reported Olga missing to the militia. I don't know how long they would've gone on searching for her if Olga herself hadn't taken the baby to the doctor's for a checkup.

"At the clinic, everybody just about died from shock. This little mommy comes in who's still wet behind the ears herself. There's no husband, no birth certificate, no nothing—not even a name. The pediatrician, a woman, really gave Olga a scolding—did everything but use swear words at her. Then she called the school. Boy, you should have seen what happened then! They forced that little fool to go back home to her mother with the baby, of course. And then they had a faculty meeting at the school. What a scandal it was. They didn't know who to fire over the incident. Then they finally settled on the gym teacher, since he of all people should've noticed her big stomach. And Olga, can you imagine, was so ungrateful. What trouble she didn't give her mother! Nastya insisted that she give the baby up for adoption. After all, Olga still had high school to finish. What would ever become of her if she didn't get a high school education? Did she think she was going to sweep floors? But Olga was having none of it. She ran away to her boyfriend's. His parents knew the whole story and took her in. Nastya kept going over there and kicking up a big fuss, but Olga started slamming the door right in her face.

"What can you say! An impudent, shameless wench! You know what she said to her so-called mother-in-law? Her boyfriend's mother made the comment that Olga's baby was so quiet, and her own son cried constantly as a baby. So Olga says to her, 'You were just too nervous during your pregnancy, that's all.' That's exactly what she said!"

The story was over. I looked around me and realized that I was on the *eliktrichka*, the commuter train. Fear crept over me—God forbid the conductor should come around now to take tickets! The train was heading toward Zelenogorsk. The two women were probably on their way to their dachas.

After finishing her story about Olga, the storyteller did not pause for a second before she launched into a description of a new dress she had bought the day before. I quickly lost interest. I stepped out between the cars to have a smoke, then got off at the next station.

On the way back to Leningrad, my seat mate was an unshaven man who was somewhat tipsy. He introduced himself as Nikolai Nikolaich, a former doctor. All the way into town, Nikolai Nikolaich chastised the intellectuals for their lack of respect for themselves. "Some lousy carpenter Fedya isn't ashamed to ask a ruble for banging in a nail. And I help his blockhead of a son to solve a math problem, and he doesn't pay me a thing for it."

He treated me to an apple, I gave him my *TV Guide,* and we became friends. Nikolai Nikolaich told me the story of why he was a failure.

"I'm a physician by profession. Gastrointestinal diseases were my specialty. I left the clinic, though, because I felt I wasn't doing the sick people any good. Just my presence alone wasn't enough at that hospital. We needed good medicines, the latest medical technology. I should have gone into research medicine right after I graduated. It was at the clinic that I started drinking heavily. Most of my colleagues worked their way up to becoming Honored Scientists,[2] thanks to their civic work. But I think a doctor shouldn't have to go around reading lectures at block committee halls. Lectures on smoking being hazardous to your health, which maybe two ancient pensioners show up to hear. Or else collecting union dues. A real doctor, or even one who just wants to gain respect, goddamn it, ought to treat the sick, and try to obtain what he needs to cure his patients, even if they don't have those medicines in his country. You get sick of the Ministry of Health finally, and you don't want to kiss ass anymore."

Nikolai Nikolaich and I said goodbye to each other on the platform of Finland Station. He left me his address and telephone number as a souvenir. I glanced at a clock and my stomach reminded me that it was time to have breakfast. Then I remembered my friend Marina was expecting me to drop in today. Marina and I have all sorts of things and problems in

2. An official Soviet title of merit.

common. I immediately cheered up at the thought of having some tea to drink at her place and then borrowing five rubles or so for groceries for the week. So off I went in search of a bus going in the direction of Petrogradskaya. On the way, a gypsy woman who was selling flowers by the train station thrust two tulips at me. I wasted sixty kopecks on them, and was left with just small change. I asked a woman passing by where I could find the bus stop (for some reason I could not get my bearings).

"You know, I don't have the slightest idea, but I think you're better off taking the metro instead," the woman answered, and it came out sounding so nicely that I started thanking her profusely and smiling broadly. Without hesitating I gave her a tulip, and saved the other for Marina.

Marina was renting a room in a communal apartment. Her neighbor, an old lady, opened the door for me and started crabbing right off. "Lord, I just don't get it, I just can't figure it out: Is it a boy or a girl? In dungarees and a cap, yet. You're here to see Marina, right?"

I spent several hours with Marina in her room. We forged her work booklet, then wondered where we could use it to get a job for Marina.[3] Marina kept saying over and over again, "Why wasn't I born a Jew? I could have left for the Wild West long ago, and over there I wouldn't be going through so much. I wouldn't be taking risks like this." She was unable to give me any tea to drink, or lend me five rubles. We racked our brains for a while to think up where we could get hold of some money, then hit upon the idea of sewing a cap. We finished the cap and went out to sell it.

It did not sell. We stood around nervously and smoked a lot.

---

3. Employees in the Soviet Union must hand in work booklets to be signed by their employers as proof of employment, and to obtain a job. A Soviet citizen who does not have a signed booklet and a job can be arrested for parasitism. Forgery of these booklets is against the law and can lead to stiff fines and imprisonment. Dissidents and others outside the system are often arrested on the charge of parasitism.

When we ran out of cigarettes, I asked some kids standing nearby if I could bum one from them. "I won't give you a cigarette, you queer!" one of them said sullenly. The boys apparently were not very perceptive if they could not tell right away that I was a girl. My painted lips along with my clothes and low voice confirmed their opinion that I was a homosexual and wanted to get acquainted. I laughed and stepped away from them.

Marina despaired of ever selling the cap. We went all over Petrogradskaya trying to sell it—to beauty parlors, cafés, and stores. But everywhere people turned us down. Then suddenly a little girl who looked like a tiny Punch traded her Pinocchio's hat for our cap, right on the street. We hung around a little then ducked into a *pelmennaya*[4] for lunch. I came out of the *pelmennaya* totally exhausted and beat. Marina walked me to my stop, split the money left over with me, and went her own way.

It took me a long time to get home, because I kept falling asleep and going in the wrong direction. In my sleep, I heard a girl exclaim, "Hey, look, that time Lenin's cloak was longer!" The bus must have been going past one of his statues.

The tiny alarm went off in my pocket. I woke up and saw my house from the bus window. "What foresight that girl has," I heard people saying behind me as I got off.

Translated by Catherine A. Fitzpatrick

4. A restaurant or snack bar where *pelmenny*, meat-filled dumplings like ravioli, are sold.

Drug Addicts

P. Z. AHMEDOVA
Samarkand, Uzbekistan

I came to Northern Palmyra from Uzbekistan to stay with
Ramsya. She had abandoned the heat of her homeland for the
fog of the Neva. Her life seemed mysterious and alluring to me.
She introduced me to her friends who took drugs. "Drug grass"
grows back home in Central Asia and people use it in the Eastern tradition. Special "pears" with a greenish pollen from "the
drug" are sold at bazaars. I had always associated the concept
of drug use with hippies, Western pop music, and rich young
people, the sons and daughters of business executives. I thought
of them as stuck-up adolescents who would work themselves
into a state of exaltation with drugs and blaring music.

Articles on this subject appeared in newspapers and magazines under the heading "The Western Mosaic." I read frequently about drug contraband—bags of heroin, marijuana,
and hashish confiscated at the borders of capitalist countries.
I read about the semilegal sale of drugs within these countries
and about fatal accidents involving the ill-starred drug addicts.
And here I found myself right in their midst, at one of their
gatherings in an apartment in Leningrad. The drug addicts
seemed exotic. As I looked around me I saw guys in worn jean
pants and jackets and young women in long, velvet skirts and
wide-brimmed hats wearing crudely fashioned aluminum
chains around their necks. They all looked emaciated and sal-
low as they shuffled around the apartment. The tape recorder
played incessantly. The drug addicts were boiling *khanka* on
a gas stove with the aid of an ordinary strainer. Next to it,
syringes were boiling in a sterilizer. I became interested in just

what *khanka* was. One of the drug addicts by the name of Igor
volunteered to instruct me on the subject. He acquainted me
with the technique of preparing the drug and with how it
worked. *Khanka* is the juice from the floret of a poppy dried
in the sun and thickened. It contains opium, which transports
the drug addicts to a state of oblivion, to their fairy-tale world
and heavenly happiness. It is customary to call half a gram of
khanka a hit. It is dissolved and boiled in three to four cubic
centimeters of water. The finished product may be injected
into the bloodstream and is divided between two drug addicts.
What does the drug addict feel after the needle is removed
from the vein? In the course of a few seconds a hot, heavy wave
rolls over the entire body causing a sensation of falling over a
precipice and of having pins and needles in the legs. This state
is known as getting off and indicates the quality of the *khanka*.
The stronger the getting-off, the better the narcotic intoxication or the high will be. The getting-off and the high vary from
one addict to another, depending on the individual's health,
temperament, and outlook on life.

I decided to try out the effects of *khanka* on myself. This
delighted the addicts, who looked upon this as a show of solidarity with them. They immediately made themselves available
to me, each wanting to be the first to take me to the world of
bliss. Someone started to make up an advertisement for drugs,
saying,

> Wind
>   rain
>   snow

can bring you down. You will feel lonely, sad, and empty down
to the depths of your very soul.

> Wind
>   rain
>   snow

will not bother you at all if you fill a syringe with *khanka* and release it into your veins. A wonderful wave of warmth will flow through your whole body. In an instant the world will be filled with the sounds of a soft, uplifting music. And a heavenly grace will descend upon you. You need to touch this serene world just once and you will long for it forever. Wipe the doubt from your mind and from your life will disappear

> Wind
>> rain
>>> snow.

I entrusted myself to Ramsya, who had led me to the apartment in the first place. With a light motion she inserted the needle into my vein and I nearly croaked. The holiday salute for November 7th flashed before my eyes.[1] I choked on a hot stream of air I had just exhaled, broke into a cold sweat, and just had time to wonder if this could be fatal before I collapsed into the abyss of unconsciousness. And on that note my voyage into wonderland came to an end. I spent the entire evening and on through the night feeling sick and vomiting, but managed not to let myself look too horrendous. By morning I had utterly worn myself out and gave myself over to chills, a hellish headache, and the exhausting process of retching. Evidently the dose had been very strong. I remained of the opinion that it is better to relieve tension through yoga. In the final analysis, each to his or her own. But my association with the drug addicts did not stop there. Without getting involved in their activities, I still wanted to get to know their way of life. Something about it interested me.

Let me begin with Ramsya. She was a native of a Central Asian republic and had spent her childhood and adolescence

1. The holiday commemorating the anniversary of the Bolshevik Revolution in 1917.

in a rural area, almost totally isolated from the civilized world. She lived with her parents at the edge of a Kazakh settlement. It was her parents, quite cultured in their own right, who gave her an ethical and aesthetic orientation in life. Ramsya became keen on literature (her father had inherited his great-grandfather's library) and she loved music and sketching. She whiled away the hours observing wild, unspoiled nature. An atmosphere of mutual understanding and participation combined with friendship and caring for one another reigned in her family home. As a little girl she was sincerely attached to her parents, appreciated and respected them, and helped them in every way she could. She gladly helped her mother tend the garden and accompanied her father on trips to the apiary. The family composed verses as a threesome and held musical gatherings in the evenings. Recognizing intelligence and talent in the child, her parents gave her free rein to make her own choices and value judgments and to spend her time as she saw fit. She had a healthy creative spirit and a mind of her own from the moment she set out on the path of independence.

Ramsya had her first collision with tyranny when she arrived in the capital city of her republic to continue her education. The dorm in which she was forced to live at the institute for applied arts required her to live in strict accordance with an elaborate set of house rules. She was never to be out later than 11:00 P.M., since they locked the doors at that time. She was never to invite guests over on weekends or Saturdays. On Sundays guests were limited to a specific amount of time and were admitted only if they left their passports with the attendant. To economize on electricity, the authorities forbid residents to have hot plates in their rooms. Instead, a cafeteria was open to students, which they called the vomitorium. Tape recorders were also forbidden, since they might disturb the quiet, working life of the students. It was against the rules to hang prints, paintings, or any other form of wall decoration that might damage the walls of the dormitory. The institute required all students to wear a uniform, to attend classes regularly, and to also attend meetings and debates on topics of ethics and morality. If you strayed from the established order, the authorities took steps against you, such as forcibly subjecting you to public reprimands and ridicule. If any further insubordination took place, they expelled the disobedient student from the institute. Upon leaving, the student would receive a nasty letter of reference, which forever closed the doors to any other educational establishment. The educational program included many subjects that have nothing to do with applied arts, for example, the history of the Communist Party of the Soviet Union, military science, and physical education. Any student exhibiting a lack of eagerness to succeed in these subjects was threatened with expulsion.

Ramsya clashed constantly with the administration of the institute and with her instructors. She found them guilty of lies, hypocrisy, and formalism. She did not get along with the head of her dormitory in particular. He was a drunkard and took bribes. For money he would organize evening festivities for his drinking crowd, using empty rooms in the dorm or even the Red Corner.[2] And why not? He was lord and master of this den. But if he noticed anyone smoking or an outsider in the dorm, he would write a damaging note about "the guilty woman" to the director of the institute. But this he did only after he had approached her with disgusting propositions for sexual relations. Ramsya was indignant, but she did not make up her mind to leave the institute. In the evenings she wandered around town nurturing plans to overthrow the director and his best friend, the dorm warden.

2. A corner within a public building or institution that contains reading material on the Communist Party, Soviet ideology, current events, and so on. There are also frequently political posters hung on the wall within this area.

On one of these walks she met two happy-go-lucky artists who distracted her from her gloomy thoughts. Without even noticing it herself, she fell in love with one of them. His name was Venyamin. He was a romantic at heart, shy, and pedantic. Happily, their feelings proved to be mutual. Venyamin became attached to his new girlfriend heart and soul, and eventually he confessed his passion for drugs. Ramsya's new friends began to take her to a patch of land outside of town that was rich in poppies and hemp. There they gathered *khanka* and *anasha*.[3] *Anasha* is also related to drugs but does not produce much intoxication on its own. It just eases the body and raises the spirits. The high from another drug increases if you smoke *anasha* when you are getting off. Ramsya would accompany her friends occasionally to the home of a Kazakh who was a longtime devotee of *anasha*. He would serve them tea and display his collection of *plan*, which is the second name for *anasha*. He described *plan* as a healer and attributed all manner of properties to it. "It makes the gloomy amusing, the jumpy calm. It inspires the songwriter and gives the timid lover the confidence of Don Juan," he would tell his guests, treating them to some *anasha*. He would smoke and sing songs with them. Meanwhile Ramsya would take a piece of paper and, in her own inimitable style, sketch the old man's face and his quarters.

Several years went by and Ramsya graduated from the institute. Her parents died one after the other. She had almost succeeded in drowning these two sorrows in drugs when a third grief visited her. Venyamin took an overdose of drugs and fatally damaged his heart. But his death did not stop Ramsya. On the contrary, she threw herself even more passionately into drugs and resolved to die while high. She even took it into her head to popularize drugs among her own

3. *Anasha* and *plan* are the Soviet equivalent of marijuana.

friends. Somehow Ramsya had gotten wind of some stories about how dealers of *khanka* and *anasha* made unbelievable profits transporting drugs from Central Asia to the country's European cities. This racket infuriated her. As soon as the season rolled around, Ramsya was out zealously harvesting *khanka* and *plan*. At the end of the harvest she would make a trip to Leningrad. She intended to "blow the drug addicts' minds" with this unexpected piece of good fortune. "The druggies in Leningrad are racking their brains every day trying to get hold of twenty-five or thirty rubles for a hit and they go through withdrawal if they can't find the money. I'll be their good fairy," thought Ramsya as she observed Leningrad from the window of a plane. In time, Ramsya herself a confirmed drug addict, became the most popular person in the Leningrad drug world. She got to know the elite. Their ranks included one Bastinda, so named for her love of the color violet; a certain Hans, possessed of a Nordic face; Andrice from one of the Baltic republics and his narcissistic friend Poop; a guy named Ragamuffin who lived illegally without documents or a fixed address; an effeminate guy named Mr. Sweet; and someone from parts not quite so distant who was called Solzhenitsyn. Everyone went by a nickname. They had been through a lot in life. Several had served time and some had even tried heroin. But no one would let Ramsya in on the secret of where their incredibly powerful drug came from. The way Ramsya saw it, the addicts of Leningrad were used to keeping their mouths shut. Truly, danger awaited around every corner. The antinarcotic division worked very effectively, and in addition to their antidrug campaign, they waged war on venereal disease. To get involved with this division meant to end up in prison. The criminal code contains an extensive article relating to drug addicts that stipulates a sentence of fifteen years behind bars. If the addict manages to get around that, he or she will definitely be sent to a psychiatric hospital or to a work-therapy dispensary. This, for all intents and purposes, is the same thing as prison—total isolation from the outside world, suspension of all rights except the right to vote, and work for the good of the homeland at half the standard wage. In the very best of circumstances, the drug addict who lands in Section 10 of the police department, where the battle against drugs is centered, is subject to police surveillance. Ramsya soon learned the importance of keeping a low profile and she openly regretted having disclosed her presence in Leningrad through her acquaintances among the elite. In the span of three weeks she had heard more than enough stories about people who went straight to prison with two-to-three-year sentences just for possession of two or three grams of *anasha*.

Ramsya went into the so-called underground just in time. On top of this she became disenchanted with a lot of the drug addicts. Not everyone understood the purposes of getting high quite as she did. In Ramsya's view, drugs exist to free people from the material world, to emancipate people, and to make possible direct contact with other people and nature, to help people understand art, and to stimulate one's sense of creativity. But for the majority of drug addicts, the high is to gratify the body, not the soul, and this makes getting high a selfish pursuit. In time, Ramsya became a solitary drug addict. Ultimately, she wants to leave Leningrad and to return to Central Asia where the life of an addict is much, much easier.

The other hero of my story is Seryoga, nicknamed Monkey because of his resemblance to a small macaque. I met Seryoga on the night I first tried *khanka*. He became addicted to drugs in a manner entirely different from Ramsya's. In his time, Seryoga had developed an inferiority complex. The reason for this was a certain ugliness. But speaking objectively, I think his face and figure were not disgusting. On the contrary, they aroused sympathy in a lighthearted way, just as one would feel sympathy for a clown. Drugs became Seryoga's reason for living, and naturally he spent all his energy on trying to get them. When Monkey got off, he would change beyond recognition. His complex would fade from his mind and this allowed him to communicate with people without constraint—chatting, joking, or getting angry. Contrary to the drug addict's established tradition of dressing originally, Seryoga's dress was absolutely traditional. But to make up for this, his way of expressing himself, his sense of humor, and his gestures were all one of a kind. He came to a drug gathering once, literally bursting in well after midnight. He immediately began to snap his fingers to the beat of the music. Without greeting anyone, he busied himself with a fluffy puppy that ran around the house pulling on everyone's clothes and inhaling the smell of *anasha*. "Come here, little furry one. You and I are going to have a little smoke," Seryoga said in a nasal voice, stretching forward his neck. Everything about his pose emphasized his protruding jaw. Monkey played with the puppy for a quarter of an hour. At the same time he rolled three joints, laughed at some of his own thoughts, or muttered to himself under his breath. Only then did he address the assembled company, "Brothers and sisters! Take these joints and listen to me. A proposal has been made to pop some red pills or 'toke' up. I've been running around all day. Half an hour ago I popped a few but I can't get off at all. I've got to catch up with you. True, my back itches. Maybe I'll rinse myself off while you boil some of that little old black *khanka*. At the same time I can steam my veins." His words should be interpreted in the following way: "My friends, help yourselves to some *anasha* and heed my words. An excellent suggestion has been made that we indulge ourselves with some caffeine or some opium. I spent the whole day looking for them for both you and me, my friends. Just half an hour ago I let myself go and took some. I had to before getting together with you. But

I just can't get off. I've got to do something about it. Damn it! I keep feeling an itch from caffeine. Here's the plan: You boil up a generous portion of *khanka* while I take a bath. And that way it will be easier for me to find my veins. Let's go! Let's get high tonight!"

Monkey set out for the bathroom but never made it. On the way he noticed me growing faint from nausea and took it upon himself to upbraid the group for their indifference: "What's the matter with you! Have you tripped out completely? This girl's about to pass out. Everyone, to her rescue!" I reassured him and thanked him for his attention, and from this moment on we established a rapport. We chatted idly for a while about various things—about the *anasha* he brought, about what steps to take in case of intense nausea, about my attractive appearance, and about communists and cops. At the last minute came a confession. Monkey drew a sad picture of how he became an unwilling participant in a drug case. His words were agitated and saturated with foul language. The shock had obviously been a strong one. Seryoga's anger arose from the arrest of two of his friends, Valentina and her underage brother Oleg, who had not anticipated a visit from the police after midnight. An unsanctioned search of the apartment was conducted and a package containing about seven hundred grams of *anasha* was discovered. Without drawing up a report of the seizure, the police dragged them off to the regional division of the police department, where they beat them up and forced Valentina to confess to possession of drugs. An investigator then concocted charges based exclusively on this one confession. In an attempt to save Oleg, Valentina assumed all responsibility. Despite her attempt, they sent Oleg to a psychiatric hospital to be cured of drug addiction without submitting him to any medical tests. The judge sentenced Valentina to four years in prison. During visits at the Kresty Prison, she cried throughout the entire block of time allotted her, cursed the humane law,[4] and, still not fully comprehending the tragedy of her situation, asked her mother to get her some fancy French-style pastries somehow. As one who had been present when the arrests were made, Seryoga was obliged to be a witness in this criminal proceeding. But he avoided implicating himself by explaining his visit to the home of the drug addicts exclusively in terms of an interest in Valentina He answered every leading question more or less by saying, "I don't know anything. I didn't see anything. You could have planted the *anasha* yourselves." Monkey had had run-ins with the police and knew one thing for sure: Never confess to anything and never sign anything. During the arrest he even had to manage to somehow slip a small package of *anasha* into the pocket of one of the policemen in the interests of his own security. But on this occasion the police were more interested in something else, namely why Seryoga was roaming about aimlessly on Budapest Street at night.

In addition to this story, Monkey talked about what life had been like in the past for Leningrad drug addicts. He told of events going back as far as five years. He reminisced about the unobstructed sale of drugs in pharmacies. All sorts of preparations containing caffeine and opium were displayed in full view on the shelves. There were all sorts of tablets, caffeine with soda, caffeine with sugar, caffeine with the herb *termopsis,* and *codterpin.*[5] In addition there was every conceivable kind of medicine for stomach ailments, some containing a mixture with opium and some made of wax capsules with opium inside. All of this was available for a few kopecks. The addicts used to buy packages of one hundred tablets and gulp down twenty-five or thirty of them before they even left the

4. The "humane law" presumably refers to the law that grants visitation privileges in prison.
5. Termopsis is an herb used to strengthen the heart. Codterpin is a cough medicine containing codeine.

pharmacy. They would float the wax capsules in a pan of boiling water, and when the liquid had cooled down and a layer of wax had formed, they would remove a film of opium from underneath. Driven by hunger for even stronger sensations (and consequently even stronger narcotics), some addicts applied for work as medical orderlies or simply established close ties with workers in medical or pharmaceutical circles. Formerly they did not keep such strict account of cocaine, *omnopon, promidol,* or morphine of hydrochlorides as they do now.[6] "Now they've turned the drug tap off," remarked Seryoga bitterly. There was a time when he considered cocaine to be the only drug worthy of the title "the pride of kings." Now there was nothing to choose from. All he could do was to choke down some homemade concoction—poppy florets ground up in a meat grinder—or to content himself with *khanka* and codeine. In recent years pharmacies had begun to require prescriptions from a doctor. Monkey was an artist in his own way: He deftly drew seals on medical documents and therefore did not lose hope.

Winter meant hard times for Seryoga. Poppies did not grow and you could not always find codeine in the drugstores. He was forced to turn to the services of those Caucasians who dealt on the drug market, secretly of course. The impudent little Georgian "pals" used youth's ever-increasing interest in drugs for their own gain. Seryoga would buy their homemade concoctions, shelling out fifteen rubles for one hundred grams, or would exchange frozen lottery bonds from the Khrushchev era called Restoration of National Agriculture. He avoided buying *khanka* and codeine. He couldn't afford them. The Georgians were charging outrageous prices for them. A single transaction consisting of perhaps three packages of codeine tablets

6. Omnopon (Pantopon) is a narcotic made from opium and used as a painkiller. Promidol is the chemical equivalent of morphine. Morphine of hydrochloride is a by-product of the manufacture of morphine.

and one tablet of *noxirona*[7] would cost the drug addict fifty rubles. (One month's salary for a cleaning woman or a nurse is between sixty and seventy rubles.) One tablet of *noxirona*, for a catalyzing and filtering effect, is independently priced at five rubles. The old maxim that it is just one step from drugs to crime comes to mind, and this maxim was not lost on Seryoga. He was an expert pickpocket, thief, and armed robber. True, he keeps his methods secret, but evidently he will not escape his gloomy fate.

I want to concentrate on how easily drugs generate criminal ideas. Within a few minutes of my arrival at a drug gathering I noticed a highly fashionable young man. I learned later that he was the organizer of the party. He was generous not only with his drugs but with all his goods. The table he had arranged looked like a luxurious still life, with fruit, sweets, and imported juices. You could see his hand everywhere. When the guests were served coffee, our host laid a pack of American cigarettes before me with a highly sophisticated gesture. He formally introduced himself and invited me to "make myself at home." His name was Andrei. I did not quite know what to make of him, since I had previously heard all sorts of unbelievable stories about him from others.

Andrei had long been certain that he had the entire drug "industry" cornered. Any shipment of hard drugs to Leningrad could not be made without his involvement. Thus when three down-and-out drug addicts turned up at his place one day and offered to treat him to some heroin, he did not pay them the slightest attention. Without seating his guests, he busied himself with hanging blinds on the windows. Maintaining this imperturbable appearance he ignored the newcomers. "Maybe where you come from they call *pentalgin*[8]

7. A sleeping pill made in Poland.
8. Pentalgin, a painkiller, is a combination of codeine, analgin, aspirin, caffeine, and sugar.

heroin!" he said sarcastically. When his guests offered to let him sample the drug, Andrei, wishing to promote his reputation as a drug addict, put the syringe into his arm without even climbing down from the stepladder he was using to hang the blinds. Two cubic centimeters of heroin knocked the proud drug industrialist from his pedestal. Andrei nearly died but he did not part with his pride. He tried to underline his superiority in every way. At drug gatherings and celebrations he alone would inject himself with morphine, "the stimulator of nobility." Yes, Andrei had more than enough "nobility." He chatted in a worldly way with everyone present, responded eagerly to everyone's requests, and tried to personally oversee each drug addict's injection, demonstrating how to insert the needle correctly. Andrei socialized with me for about ten minutes. He spent the entire time in a monologue on the characteristics of various drugs: *Khanka* is a bold, businesslike drug. It's good for household chores and for . . . adventures. Codeine is suited to petty, pathetic little people who need to free themselves from their groveling and their wretched, lowly essence, for a little while at least. Morphine and cocaine are the kings of drugs. They elevate one above the world and purify the soul." He did not let me get a word in edgeways and he never doubted the accuracy of his evaluations for a minute. I learned about this arrogant drug addict's social position and about the nature of his activities from fragments of conversations between his friends. It turned out that Andrei was a so-called parasite, ostensibly an invalid schizophrenic.[9] His parents occupy rather important posts in the police system.

Andrei is a professional con artist, a specialist in "envelopes." He also makes a little money on the side from speculating in

9. In Soviet society, people without officially registered work are labeled parasites. This term can be applied to any person living outside official society, from drug addicts to nonconformist artists to those living unregistered and illegally in the large cities.

currency and merchandise. He began every morning with *khanka*. This would bring him around to a state of readiness. He would select a "work site" on the map, perhaps a department store, and go there with envelopes that had been specially prepared earlier. In some of these envelopes there were pieces of paper the size of paper money in various denominations. These are known in the criminal world as dolls. Andrei would leave the other envelopes empty. In the department store it was not hard to find someone who needed an item that was out of stock, such as a fur-lined overcoat. Andrei would get acquainted with a likely simpleton and offer to help, presenting himself as a powerful figure in the trade world. He was possessed of a certain charm and his involvement gave every appearance of being sincere. The fur-lined overcoat that he wore also played its role. When he was satisfied that he had won the buyer's trust and the buyer was ready to purchase a fur-lined overcoat, Andrei would get down to business. From his briefcase he would take out a magazine that contained all the envelopes. He would then select an empty envelope and insist that the buyer put his money inside it. Andrei would quote a price quite a bit higher than the normal asking price for the item in question. This detail of pricing was essential to create an impression of authenticity, because the buyer is already psychologically prepared to pay more than the regular price for the item and a low price would raise people's suspicions. The buyer expects to be charged extra for the unofficial transaction. Andrei had learned his black market techniques well. To make everything look plausible he would explain very carefully where the buyer was to go and with whom he should speak. For example, he might tell him to go to the department store warehouse; he would have already written the name of a fictitious manager of the warehouse on the envelope and would have signed his name as the person who made the recommendation. After switching envelopes with the sleight of hand of a magician, he would place the doll into the hands of the trusting buyer. After two or three of these operations, Andrei's billfold would be bulging with money.

Things did not always go smoothly. Occasionally people suspected foul play; other times Andrei would get lazy and would not prepare a neat-looking doll, which then might appear crumpled or torn at the edges. This gave him away instantly. But Andrei was not afraid of risks or failure. He knew that the police would hardly refuse a bribe. And even if they were to refuse, his parents would always come to the rescue. Andrei was their cherished little flower. From time to time they would give him large sums of money so that he "would not be naughty" anymore and would not end up at the police station. He had a passion for the hunt and pursued it in one way or another. He was always searching for new methods of making money. Sometimes he would go to the market and buy drugs wholesale with the idea of reselling them. Other times he chased foreigners: In his view they alone could satisfy the taste of a cultivated person. Lowering himself, Andrei would solicit various goods from Finns who are constant visitors to Leningrad. They come to entertain themselves on their days off. He would ask them for jeans, shirts, chewing gum, cigarettes, and plastic bags. If the Finns laughed at him and refused to give him things as presents, Andrei offered them vodka or friendly young women in exchange. The good life was the only thing he cared about. Among his friends Andrei felt like a professor of business and pleasure. Like an idol, he organized parties for the hungry and thirsty. On such occasions the drug addicts would forget about the everyday cruelty of the profiteer.

Translated by Rebecca Park

The Woman and Prison: A Conversation with Galina Zlatkina and Valeriya N.

GALINA GRIGORYEVA
Leningrad, Russia

It is well known that the condition of any society is most clearly characterized by its "prisons, barracks, and hospitals," to quote one of our poets. Fortunately, there are not barracks for women yet, but almost every woman has surely had the opportunity to acquaint herself with hospitals. But prison— that is something else.

I drew the information cited here from numerous conversations with Galina Zlatkina and her friend Valeriya. Galina is twenty-three and was imprisoned for one year. The first three months she spent at the Crosses, which is an investigation-isolation prison in Leningrad built in the form of crosses, and the remaining term she spent in the prison camp in Sablino, a general regimen corrective labor camp. Valeriya, age twenty, is Galina's friend from the Crosses and had spent half a year there.

I ask that the information presented in this interview be regarded not as the "dissemination of false information" [1] that "defames" someone, but as a transcript of private conversations, personal, subjective opinions, and an eyewitness evaluation, because published information of this sort is not available.

Q. For what reasons do women end up in prison most often? What kind of women are they?

1. This is a reference to Article 190 of the R.S.F.S.R. Criminal Code, which is often used to imprison dissidents in the Soviet Union.

193

A. Approximately 80 percent of all the women we met in prison were thirty years old or younger. Many of them are serving time for parasitism, that is, for not having worked for several months. Then there are the so-called *bomzhi*.[2] Other prevalent penal code articles for which women are sentenced read: "Refusal to receive medical treatment" and "Refusal to be checked for venereal disease." There are also Soviet gypsies who are in prison for swindling, pickpocketing, and robbing apartments. The most common term of imprisonment is one to three years.

Q. How do women become bomzhi?

A. Some of them, for the most part young women, go off limits, which was the case with me. What that means is leaving your place of work, where you are given a residence permit and a dormitory. If a person goes off limits, he or she loses the right to go to another place of work that also has a limit. You can't or don't want to go back home to the provinces, so you stay in the city at loose ends. You struggle somehow to find a job and to get registered. In Leningrad, this is very difficult, even though there are Help Wanted signs all over the place. If a person in this situation is detained by the police during a regular document check, he or she is given an order to leave the city within the next three days. After three such detentions, the person is subject to imprisonment for one year, for violation of passport laws and vagrancy.

Q. Let's go back to the charge "refusal to accept medical treatment." Why does that happen?

2. *Bomzhi* is the Russian acronym for "without a definite place of residence."

A. For the most part, "refusal" means failure to show up to have samples taken and lab tests performed. Often people are sent to dispensaries at their previous place of residence and for various reasons they can't go back there. Furthermore, a woman who comes down with syphilis, let's say, is treated with contempt, as if she were a criminal or a prostitute, and this humiliating treatment naturally causes the unfortunate person, who is already unhappy enough, to avoid these medical institutions.

Q. *You mentioned that you came across pregnant women in prison. Are these homeless* bomzhi?

A. Not necessarily. A pregnant woman can be arrested and put in jail under any charge, and sometimes she even discovers that she's pregnant while she's in prison. "It doesn't matter, don't worry," the prison gynecologist says soothingly. "Beautiful, healthy babies are born here in the Crosses!"

Up until their fifth month, the women are kept on the regular prison diet (which comes to thirty-seven kopecks a day per person). After the twentieth week of pregnancy, the food is somewhat improved.

When the time comes for the woman to give birth, she is taken to the maternity hospital under guard, and while she's giving birth, the guards wait in the hall. If a woman is in prison for a more serious crime, guards may attend the birth. After the woman has given birth and rested for the necessary two hours, she is immediately taken back to prison and put in a room in the hospital section with her newborn baby. In this room, several women with children wash their laundry, feed the children, cook, smoke, and perform their daily functions. Two-hour walks are taken in the courtyard, which is covered with iron rods—it's called the cage.

After serving their time in the Crosses women with babies are sent to a special prison camp, where the women work and the children are kept in a separate area and are brought to the mothers for feedings. If the term of punishment is long enough —five, six, or more years—the woman is usually forced to give up her child, and is deprived of her maternal rights, either voluntarily or under pressure.

Do you remember last New Year's? At the time there was a severe frost, the temperature was minus 40° F. We knew that women with children were being transferred long distances to the east in unheated vans. And this was during the "Year of the Child."

Q. Tell me about prison regulations—food, visitation rights, punishment, and so on.

A. The usual cell is designed for twelve people. But the cells are overcrowded and there are twenty to thirty people in them. And since there are only twelve folding cots in the rooms, some women must lie on the floor or under the cots. There are both types of lice, the kind that stay in your clothes and head lice.

Food is served three times a day. Breakfast consists of porridge, hot water for tea, fifteen grams [less than an ounce] of sugar, and half a kilo [one pound] of special low-grade bread —for the entire day. During lunch prisoners get soup with strands of meat, noodles that are like paste, and no main course. Dinner is vegetable ragout or fish soup, which is called the grave because there are fish skeletons in it.

Visits are allowed once every four months, for two hours. Conversations are allowed with a maximum of two close relatives across a glass wall. Personal visits are allowed every six months for one to three days, depending on how far away the relatives live. Fiancés and cohabitants don't count as relatives. Marriages can be registered in prison, for which representatives from the marriage license bureau are sent. After registering the marriage, the newlyweds are given three days to live together in a special room, where they are allowed a few comforts, such as a little kitchen.

Medical care. Nurses come to the cells once every three days to give the women small quantities of cotton [to use as sanitary napkins], and the women must openly demonstrate their need in order to get the cotton.

GALINA ZLATKINA'S STORY

Our cell, which contained thirty-eight women, went on a hunger strike, demanding that the administration improve our living conditions. I should point out that if only one or a few prisoners in a cell go on a hunger strike, no one will pay any attention to them, because the administration figures that the other women are surely giving them food on the side. But this time it was the entire cell! We demanded that the following inconveniences be changed: the lack of ventilation in the cells; the cutting of rations because of overcrowding; the scarcity of medical attention (the nurse came only once every three days, and prisoners couldn't call a doctor); the infrequency of showers (once a week, four at a time for ten minutes, which meant two and a half minutes per person); and the treatment by the guards, who could strike the women with their bunches of keys or swear at them. Most likely, they suspected me and two other women of organizing the hunger strike.

Since we were the initiators, we were summoned by the administration, but we insisted on continuing the strike. After a little while, the three of us were put in a solitary confinement cell, with a more severe regimen. I was presented with a paper that stated that I was to be put in the punishment cell for five days. I was supposed to sign the paper, but I refused, knowing that my signature on the document would give them a way of adding more days. In the punishment cell a prisoner is fed every other day, the quota being cut to one third (which costs about twenty-four kopecks). On the fast days, sometimes you are given bread and water. I went on a hunger strike in the punishment cell, as the only possible form of protest. I was told, "You don't have to eat, but take the food anyway." I kept returning the dishes with the untouched food. After six days of hunger strike, intravenous feeding usually begins. After I had served my five days in the punishment cell, I was returned to my cell. Everything was left just as it had been before.

VALERIYA'S STORY

I wound up in the punishment cell for ten days, for a similar reason. I had expressed my indignation with the fact that the administration and the guards were arbitrarily making the prison regimen even more severe than it already was. It was that same cold winter with the minus 40°F temperature. And the ventilation was turned on in the cell, to muffle the conversations, which created an additional draft. During the day you could warm up a little bit by the radiator, but at night the radiator was turned off, supposedly because of technical difficulties.

In the Crosses the prisoners wore their own clothing, but in the punishment cell we were given special clothes: a cotton dress, pants without elastic, and also something like a pillowcase with straps—a "nightgown," which barely covered your belly button.

The folding cots were put out at ten o'clock at night and folded up at six o'clock in the morning, but it was impossible to use them. It was terribly cold in the cell, below freezing, and all night you'd try to get warm, curling up and pulling your "pillowcase" over your legs. I don't remember exactly, but on either the fourth or fifth day I couldn't hold out any longer, and lost consciousness. As I fell, I hit my elbow against an uneven place in the wall and it bled. I woke up all bloody and somehow made it to the radiator.

After I was released from prison and finally made it home, I lay in critical condition for a month and a half, with a temperature above 104° F. I found myself also at death's door, and was delirious with prison nightmares. Only several months later did I finally get better.

Q. It is no secret to anyone that homosexuality is prevalent in men's prisons, and it is often of an aggressive nature. What is it like in women's prisons?

A. Many women in the outside world become disappointed with men. A spiritually weak, drunk, corrupt man isn't capable of strong feelings, or of having a true and heartfelt relationship. Besides, the complete isolation from the outside world and the infrequency of visits force women to get involved in a unique prison vacuum, with an unavoidable assimilation to its internal order. I am referring to love between women, to so-called lesbianism.

Q. What sorts of lesbian relationships are there, and do many women prisoners participate in them?

A. No. Less than half the women are involved in lesbian love in one way or another. The administration forbids and punishes such practices, considering them to be a form of corruption, but without any results. Almost all the young people, who are sent to penal colonies for minors, have a lot of experience in love relationships between women. The other half of the women who don't take part in such activities are divided into those who sympathize and those who condemn lesbianism.

Q. How do the women find each other?

A. Through mutual liking, inclination, love. The "tops" [the women who play the role of the man] are usually more experienced, maintaining a male standard of behavior, and gradually their psychological traits become intensified in this direction.

You shouldn't think that these relations are pursued just for sexual gratification. The satisfaction is usually in the feeling of friendship. There really is love between lesbians, often very demanding love, reaching the point of very severe jealousy. The relationships between women are sometimes kept after they are let out of prison.

Q. And my last question to you: How would you like to go on living?

A. There are the same problems—finding a place to live, finding work, which becomes even more difficult after having been in prison. But we don't want to repeat our prison experience. It would be better to leave the country.

Translated by Catherine A. Fitzpatrick

Women and the State

Soviet women have for the most part been reliable and loyal servants of the state. Given a degree of legal equality unprecedented in world society, they have flocked into the paid labor force and overcome high pre-revolutionary illiteracy rates to overtake and surpass Soviet men in average years of formal education. In times of crisis, most notably during World War II, women performed their traditional domestic duties, raised the children, staffed the factories and farms, and, when necessary, served as combat troops, pilots, and in other military roles.

The impressive legal guarantees of equality do not translate into reality at the level of political decision-making. Although intensive efforts at recruitment have brought female party membership up to 25 percent, women are very sparsely represented at the top of the power structure. Since the war, two women have held ministerial posts; none do so at present. Similarly, no women sit on the Politburo, and women represent about 4 percent of all Central Committee members. Three key power centers, the secret police, the military, and the diplomatic corps, have very few women in their ranks. Those areas in which women are more numerous, such as health, cultural affairs, social security, and consumer services, are often short-changed in terms of overall budget priorities.

The Soviet Woman: Support and Mainstay of the Regime

ALLA SARIBAN
Leningrad, Russia

Women in the Soviet Union have more obligations than men and have far more difficult lives. That much is obvious. After all, even leaving aside such subjects as the moral state of Soviet society with its prevailing customs and general atmosphere (and, in my opinion, this is precisely why women are beaten in Russia and why they have been reduced to their present state), there remains at least one objective and completely "material" index of their oppressed state. That index is the work they are forced to do. Without a doubt the Soviet woman is the object of colossal exploitation by society, much more so than is the Soviet man.

After all, the majority of women here are forced to work for the government and spend as much time on the job as do men. And it is not because everyone is eager to work. It is simply that if they did not, they would not be able to make ends meet. Women's salaries constitute an essential contribution to the family budget. But, as is well known, Soviet women's main work begins after official working hours are over. That is when they start on the housework and the everyday business of living. These are very difficult tasks indeed. Groceries are in short supply, there are lines everywhere, and service for the consumer is horrifying. The merest trifle becomes a problem. Housework requires a tremendous expenditure of time and energy, and creates a great deal of tension. Small wonder that women say they rest up from their household duties while at their government jobs. In recent years traditional women's work has become much more difficult and there is every indication that it will continue to become so. Prices are rising, groceries and goods are becoming more and more scarce, and service for the customer becomes more unbearable with each day. In addition, the subject of widespread thievery and the system of influence is becoming too horrifying to even discuss.

Characteristically, as hard as the household work is, it is as if society does not consider it work at all but rather something low, second-class, and unworthy of respect. Women not only do not receive any respect for their work (to say nothing of material compensation) but rather are subjected to social contempt as creatures of a lower order whose very nature dictates that they should do the dirty work.

Soviet women's position is the natural result of the social and economic laws and the ideology of the Soviet system. These are the sources of our tragedies in life, of the unnatural, neurosis-creating position in which we find ourselves. This position represses and deforms the best sides of our nature. This is precisely why the majority of Soviet women do not live but perish alive, without the opportunity to realize their potential as individuals, as women, and as members of society.

For example, one of the reasons for the contemptuous attitude toward women and their very real degradation in Soviet society was the ideological indoctrination of the Soviet people. In the course of several years the idea has been instilled in people that the only "real" life, the only life worthy of a human being, is a life dedicated to the task of building a new society. To work on this great construction project, to launch rockets—that is what life is really all about. Day-to-day living, the home, cooking—all these concerns are petit bourgeois. A person is valued in society only as a producer. One's private life, everyday lives, marital relations, and the like are considered lowly and shameful, like defecation. It is no wonder that a negative attitude toward a person's private life (including traditionally female activities) took root firmly in society.

As far as the actual economic conditions under which women suffer are concerned, there are at least three reasons for them at the root of the Soviet system. In the first place, the Soviet economy develops heavy industry for the most part; the "production of the means of production" [1] are the military industry. Relatively little attention is paid to the "production of goods for immediate use," which means goods for people. In the second place, no one bothers to study the interests and needs of the people, so they are not taken into account in economic planning. This policy means the total neglect of people's needs for the sake of other goals. And third, the Soviet system is inefficient and inflexible. By its very nature it is so poorly adapted to the requirements of creating goods of quality and variety, so incapable of keeping up with the demand for one thing or another, that even if the authorities had the very best of intentions, they would hardly be able to create good living conditions for a large segment of the population.

The Soviet system's planned economy in no way facilitates the normal flow of life. On the contrary, it has a clear tendency to complicate a simple life in every possible way, to pressure and to disorganize. This is exactly why traditional women's work in Soviet society is, essentially, a never-ending, intensive, dramatic struggle against a plurality of factors, all of which hinder women in successfully getting their work done. Anyone can have a job working for the government (and everyone does). But you cannot actually make housework your full-time, official job. And housework is truly a

---

1. The author is using Marxist terminology here to make her point that the Soviet economy concentrates on creating factories and equipment to increase production instead of meeting consumer needs.

matter of survival. After all, if I, as a woman, do not do all the essential things—the shopping, the cleaning, the laundry —who will do them? And if nobody does them, what are you going to do—die? So, like it or not, you do them.

Thanks to the titanic efforts of Soviet women, a simple, functioning system is maintained in stable condition. Normal human life goes on, however poorly. These titanic efforts are the cement that holds society together, preventing its total collapse. This is how the Soviet woman, by virtue of all the things she does in life, has become one of the most important supports of the existing regime. Let us consider a ridiculous idea for a moment. What if Soviet women were to refuse to do the housework, were to "commit sabotage," as people are accustomed to doing on their government job. What would happen? Look around you: people would be keeling over before a month was up, everyone, that is, except the people's servants.[2]

There is another, less obvious, but nevertheless important reason why women are a strong, reliable support of the present Soviet regime. The crux of the matter is this: Soviet women, in some inner part of their beings, frequently without being aware of it, have a distinct tendency to make common cause with the Soviet system and to identify with it. This is not very obvious, but as far as I have observed, this is unfortunately the case.

All Soviet people are dissatisfied with the status quo and curse it. Women curse it no less actively than men. In fact, women even exceed men in this, since women have more reasons to curse. Yet if you listen carefully and think about what they are saying, you find that rarely do any of their complaints turn into an outright rejection of the system itself. They may complain about people in power who enjoy various privi-

2. The phrase "the people's servants" generally refers to government officials.

leges, about their work and moral habits. They may complain about specific things that have been done wrong or not at all. They may even complain about the Soviet system as a whole. But you will rarely hear them reject the Soviet system outright.

The things that women have to criticize and complain about are things that they deal with on an immediate, everyday basis. And even if a discussion does progress to general topics, in the majority of cases it assumes a day-to-day character. If the discussion is conducted on a rational level, it rarely gets far enough along to include common principles. If the discussion is conducted on a psychological level, then it rarely encompasses spiritual or existential topics.

The average Soviet woman's consciousness, and even to a significant degree her unconscious, are rigidly confined to the everyday world. There are several reasons for this. The first is that the practical life of Soviet women, and for that matter of all Soviet people, is limited to everyday concerns much more so than is that of people in democratic countries. For nothing in Soviet society depends on the individual. No one and no thing takes him or her into account. People do not even have any illusions that their opinions count for something or that anyone is listening to them. The only sphere of activity within their own world and the world around them in which people have some degree of influence (and even this is very limited) is the sphere of the day-to-day. Here they can make some choices and decisions. They can decide what to get, what to buy, what to do. And then, of course, there is a person's job, but that is a special subject I will not go into here.

The second reason is simply that the average Soviet woman does not have the time, the strength, or the inner psychological reserves to think of anything other than the immediate, the close at hand, and the day-to-day.

Third, in order to look at life from a wide perspective and see beyond the hustle and bustle of your immediate surroundings, you need psychological practice and a "normal" ideology that is adapted to life. The average Soviet has neither of these things. The majority of world views instilled in our society has a surprisingly nonvital, abstract character. They instinctively reject the everyday consciousness and have no influence on it whatever. But most important, the Soviet woman materialist is not capable of rising above everyday cares and finding in life any meaning or goals beyond the limits of earthly needs.

The Soviet woman, whose attention is constantly occupied by her immediate surroundings, finds herself defenseless against attacks by the Soviet propaganda machine. By a well-known law of psychology, a person gets used to the oft-repeated statement and no longer actively thinks it through in his or her own mind but relates to it with total indifference. And almost without noticing it, he or she internalizes it and gradually it takes root in the subconscious and becomes a firm belief. In the same way Soviet women hardly notice the slogans hanging everywhere. They let much of what they hear on television and the radio "in one ear and out the other." And yet those same slogans are hanging everywhere and women continue to do their housework to the drone of radio and television.

It is not always easy to see how propaganda has affected Soviet women, since it is rarely possible to persuade them to talk about anything other than the practical and the day-to-day (even if this may include politics, morality, and the like). But if you have managed to persuade them to talk about ideas and questions of principle, keep it up! Then you might really hear something!

I have often been able to talk women out of their beliefs by forcing them to express their opinions on common topics like responsibility or personal and civic duty. As a rule, my "damn questions" caught them unprepared. They almost always became confused. It seemed as though they had not given the questions much thought until then. Their answers were almost always quite incoherent and contained the most varied and often contradictory assertions. Yet within this hodgepodge, there were often traces of an unconditional faith in the fairness of certain assertions made by Soviet propaganda. These assertions, it would seem, needed fools for an audience. Who believed which assertion depended on the individual.

But the main reason Soviet women get caught by the propaganda fishing line is that people want to believe in something. They want to see some kind of goal and meaning in life. Not only is there nothing ideal in the lives of Soviet women, there is not even much simple beauty. Everything is earthbound, banal, and gray. But the human soul thirsts for the ideal, the lofty. It knows that another rich, full, "real" life exists, and it longs for it and thirsts to join in that rich, full life.

Everything in life that is beautiful, real, and ideal is usurped by Soviet propaganda and replaced by the ideals of love for the Soviet Union, work for the good of the country, the construction of a better future, and so on and so on.

People get caught in the Soviet propaganda trap, which is set up as follows: The propaganda machine takes the concept of love for the homeland and the craving for involvement in a project that will benefit people and binds them inseparably with dedication to the Soviet system in its present form and the moral necessity of supporting that system in the face of outside danger and of working selflessly for Soviet power. People have very little information about anything other than Soviet life, and as sad as that may be, they fall to one degree or another into this trap. They fall into it despite their own disappointment with the system, despite their own personal experience and their observations of things around them.

Women are especially susceptible to this trap. In addition to craving ideals and a meaning for life, the Soviet woman strives desperately to find justification for the sufferings she is condemned to. She knows that her sufferings are the result of the system. But she also knows that she does not have the strength to change the Soviet regime. It is senseless to be indignant: You still will not change anything. You will not change Soviet life and you will not even change your own. You will just have to put up with it!

The total certainty that one can change nothing is characteristic of the consciousness of the Soviet people. But the thought that their sufferings are without purpose or meaning is intolerable. Anyone can participate in the theater of the absurd, which is what Soviet life is, and not despair or go mad. And there are people who do go mad, all the while telling themselves things that, through their own personal experience and elementary common sense, it would seem absolutely impossible to believe.

The sufferings that Soviet people experience are real. And they want to believe that the causes for these sufferings are worthy. Consequently they may say, "We live poorly and are unhappy because the imperialists have stirred everything up. We must strengthen our defense." Or, "We have nothing to eat because our country is so good that it helps everyone; and if it didn't help everyone, the whole world would be won over to the side of the imperialists."

And the more difficult the sufferings become, the more intense becomes the craving to believe that these sufferings arise from worthy causes. As a result, it is difficult to say what is going to happen in the future. Life keeps getting harder and the Soviet propaganda has been stepped up—and, in a sense, it has become more sophisticated.

We, the participants of the Russian feminist movement, are doing everything in our power to change the situation that I have described above. We are trying to explain to Soviet women the real state of affairs and to tell them the truth.

But our opportunities to act on the minds and souls of our

fellow countrywomen are few. We cannot compete with a system that consciously keeps its people in a state of ignorance and has effective means to prevent the dispersal of any information inside the Soviet Union that is unfavorable to it.

We cannot compete with the huge, sophisticated propaganda machine that systematically poisons people with lies.

We will be able to accomplish something on the condition that we receive wide support from communities abroad. Free people of the West must recognize clearly that their silence on the situation within the Soviet Union contributes materially and spiritually to the slavery of the Soviet people and especially of Soviet women.

Communities of the West must constantly remember their oppressed Eastern sisters and brothers. And as often as possible, at every semblance of an opportunity, they must express their disapproval of the Soviet system.

Translated by Rebecca Park

A Discussion with the KGB

TATYANA MAMONOVA
Leningrad, Russia

The discussion took place in the regional committee office in a luxurious detached house near the Anichkov Bridge, Leningrad, 1979.

"Do you know why you are here?"
Two men, approximately my age, are leading the discussion. The first one is named Efimov and the second one is introduced to me as Comrade.
"I haven't the slightest idea."
"Think about it. Perhaps you will remember why we have become interested in you *again*."
"You have your reasons. Anything could be a reason. Last time, for example, they questioned me in connection with the collector Georgi Mikhailov, who was keeping my artwork."
"Well, but if we return to the early seventies."
"It was just at that time that I was beginning to exhibit my work with the nonconformists. Everyone knows that."
"And you weren't planning to publish a feminist journal at that time?"
One man is sitting in one corner, the second in another corner. Evidently this was supposed to make me feel as though I were under cross fire.
"Somehow I don't recall it."
"As far as we know you were contemplating it even *then*."
"Curious. Well, I didn't know that."
I search my memory. Where did they come up with this? As far back as the 1960s they have questioned me in connection

215

with my friend from Moscow, Y. Nikolayeva, who had recently written a book called *Those Who Have Betrayed Hippocrates* about the misuse of psychiatric hospitals. And then, hoping to persuade me of the noble role of the KGB, they directed my attention to their recent exposure of a fascist youth organization that was publishing its own journal. To this I could have answered, "Maybe it isn't worth it to forbid youth to express themselves. Maybe if they were allowed to speak freely, all the alien ideas would disappear of their own accord. I, in particular, would also not refuse to publish a journal, since the status of women concerns me." But I did not say this to them.
"You don't deny that you are the publisher and editor of the journal *Woman and Russia*."
"I don't deny it. I am glad that from the day we signed the Helsinki Accords in 1975 we have finally been given the opportunity to give and receive information."
"You are publishing *dis*information. Aren't you ashamed? This pathetic little book . . ."
The more respectable-looking comrade places the worst copy of our book in front of me and I breathe a sigh of relief, thinking, "Thank God they got hold of the worst-looking copy!" Piecing everything together, I concluded that they had intercepted the book at customs in Moscow from a selfless older American woman with whom Tatyana Goricheva had shared an interest in Christianity.
"We'll try to make the next issue look better."
"Why don't you publish officially?"
"I'm prepared to have the second volume published officially. Will you help us?"
"That is not within our scope."
"To help? Then you mean you only punish?"
"Why didn't you try to get published officially?" Pointing to our book, "It would be in your best interests!"
"Sure, and it's in my best interests to be here having fun with

you instead of going to the puppet theater with my four-year-old son. And I *have* made official attempts more than once. I even corresponded with the editor in chief of the journal *Women of the World* for several years."

"You also worked for television and wrote for *Komsomolskaya Pravda,* but it didn't work out."

"I don't see what you're gloating about."

"But they were helping you."

"I'm not so sure."

"Your articles were published in *Aurora.*"

"I left *Aurora* because I couldn't get any satisfaction."

"You could have chosen a means to conduct the struggle."

"Well, right now this is the means I have chosen."

"You picked yourself a great bunch of people: Yulia Voznesenskaya, a criminal; Tatyana Goricheva, a hysterical woman; Sophia Sokolova, a hack writer; Natalya Malakhovskaya, a little fool who hurts her own child."

"My evaluations don't exactly coincide with yours. As far as Natalya's child is concerned, the conditions in which he lives are hurting him. The two of them live in a tiny little room with a ceiling that has caved in and no one will fix it. Would you like to go there now and take a look? You'll see what I mean."

"That's an isolated case. But women have made many gains under Soviet rule."

"Sure, now they can fly to outer space or become the minister of culture. But in sixty-two years women of the West have achieved more and they have done so without a socialist revolution."

"You wanted to become a housewife but others have achieved more. You could have gone to one government office or another."

"Malakhovskaya went to one government office or another. She even wrote a letter to Brezhnev, but her ceiling is still in its same pathetic state. So it's unlikely that they would pay much attention to me, a housewife, in government offices."

"Well, of course, Brezhnev is not about to get involved in this. There are deputies for that and many women among them."

"Will you introduce me to them?"

"I'm not acquainted with any of them."

"I'm not either."

"Ok, so you're not satisfied. But what sort of concrete proposals do you have?"

"I submit my candidacy for government office."

"Who are you to hand down judgments and run things?"

"For me the highest judge is my conscience."

"Your conscience isn't clean."

"That's your opinion."

"The people have to nominate you, an organization!"

"So we'll get the people together. We'll create an organization. There are plenty of people who support me."

"But the organization must be official."

"So make it official! And then Lenin's bright hope that 'the cook will run the government' will finally be fulfilled."

One man steps out for a cigarette, but the other remains.

"Do you really want to hold office?"

"Why not?"

"I suppose you see yourself as a representative of the people's will."

"Of course."

The second one returns.

"I don't hesitate to call you an agent provocateur."

"So don't hesitate, don't hesitate!"

"Do you intend to carry on?"

"Carry on what?"

"The journal, feminism."

"I would be involved in feminism no matter where I lived.

And I will express my thoughts in the future wherever I happen to be."

"Think about your child."

"That's exactly whom I'm thinking of first and foremost. I propose to convert all ideological buildings into nursery schools and maternity homes. I've already got one picked out on Smolny Passage." [1]

"Yulia Voznesenskaya didn't think about her children."

"It was you that didn't think about her children."

"She was convicted by Soviet law!"

"Soviet law allowed mistakes so often in the Stalin era that it could be mistaken even now."

"You participate in elections."

"For the time being we all participate in elections, until we really get to thinking."

"As distinct from you, other people vote consciously."

"Yeah, they drag some poor devil from his lousy little drinking hole and he *consciously* drops the scrap of paper in the urn and goes back to his drinking hole."

"It isn't just drunkards who vote, but also young people, students. By the way, your Goricheva is clouding some weak students' brains. Because of her, students are dropping out of institutes!"

"That means she has the strength of her convictions."

"She's holding seminars that no one needs."

"You'd do better to outlaw some of those drinking holes than seminars. Those who don't want to don't have to go to seminars. I don't go myself. But I respect Goricheva and I'm sure that she is incapable of teaching young people bad things

1. The author is suggesting that they turn the Smolny Convent into a nursery or maternity home. The Smolny Convent was Lenin's headquarters at the time of the October Revolution and is now a museum devoted to the Revolution.

because she is a good and deeply spiritual person. She never refuses her friends help. Holding seminars is her personal right."

"You're always talking about rights, but you forget about obligations."

"On the contrary, all I've had up to now are obligations, but now, finally, the Helsinki Accords have given us rights. Article 19 . . ."

"Is Article 19 the only article you like?"

"No, I also like Article 13 of the Helsinki Accords."

"And the legal code? The constitution?"

"I prefer to think on a global scale. But I don't think Soviet legal documents contradict foreign legal documents. They've been signed by the same person."

"What person?"

"Our government."

"But why do you want to conceal your activities by publishing your writings under pseudonyms?"

"If you'll give me a forum, I'll say everything I've had printed under pseudonyms right out in the open."

"Do you want to leave this country?"

"I would like to see the world, the earth on which I was born, just like you or any other person."

I remember a friend of mine applied for permission to visit some friends in Hungary. "Why don't you go to Lake Baikal," the Visa and Registration Department told her after they refused to grant her request. I, alas, have traveled far and wide throughout the country and have seen everything. I have been to Kamchatka alone several times.

"Seeing the world is one thing, but leaving the country is another. You know that."

"If I have the chance to travel freely all over the world, that will suffice. Then it won't be necessary to *leave*."

"Do you think it's better over there?"

"I'm not in a position to judge. I've never been there. But based on certain facts, I'm inclined to think so."

"Well, it seems we've gotten nowhere. You've stuck to your positions and we to ours. Will you write down your goals and tasks for the journal *Woman and Russia* for us?"

"No."

"If we write them, will you sign?"

"No, because I can't be sure that you won't misinterpret my words."

"Then with your permission, we will invite you back again."

"And if I don't give you my permission?"

"Then we'll get a court order" (this from the smaller of the two interviewers). "We'll prevail upon you from a position of strength, if you know what I mean. Are you planning to inform the diplomats?"

"I refuse to answer."

Translated by Rebecca Park

About the Almanac

NINA YARINA
Leningrad, Russia

It was with great enthusiasm that I viewed the appearance of the first free feminist publication in our country, and I suppose that my attitude agrees with that of the majority of women in Russia: It's about time!

Truly, each of us is surrounded by such a plurality of problems, frequently unsolvable, that we sometimes just want to lie down and die.

It would be wrong to say that the official press has passed over women's problems in silence. Problems of one sort or another relating to women are constantly being discussed: for example, the combining of women's roles at home and at work; problems of marriage; difficulties with a family and raising children. Lately the mass media have even ventured, albeit cautiously, to write an occasional piece about the intimate side of relations between the sexes. But after examining the character of the published materials and the special angle with which our concerns are examined, I have concluded that it is useless to expect an honest illumination and an unhypocritical discussion of them in the official press. The reason for this is buried, evidently, in the official press's overall method of working on the minds of the people ideologically. Much has been written about that and it does not bear repeating. As far as women's problems are concerned, it is possible to extract from the given reading material only false assumptions and impractical schemes that, if taken seriously, can only further complicate and entangle our lives.

Therefore, a publication dedicated to women's problems,

free of the officially established falseness and hypocrisy that permeates our society is imperative in my opinion.

The main goal of the publication should be to familiarize readers with the modern views of women. Otherwise no one will know anything about them. It would also be valuable, insofar as it is possible, for the *Almanac* to participate in the development of the idea of feminism, paying special attention to our experience, which is in some ways unique.

For us this is of paramount importance, because our women are the victims of an absolutely perverted understanding of their nature, destiny, and capabilities. This perverted understanding of the nature of women—our curse—is the basic reason for our inner lack of freedom. It spoiled the best years of my life and, as far as I can observe, continues to spoil the lives of many women. The distorted and humiliating view of women found everywhere does not constitute a theatrical concept but rather represents a special point of view, a way of viewing things, a specific psychological direction. I do not want to dwell on this, since I consider it a different, large topic. I consider an elaboration and working out of this topic to be an extremely interesting and instructive activity, and the more people who study it, the better off we shall be. It is all the more interesting because the distorted understanding of the nature of women specific to our country is prevalent almost everywhere over here, despite the differences in living conditions, culture, and so on within the various groups of our country's huge population. This understanding was produced simultaneously, of its own accord, and was by no means the result of one individual's ill will. The immediate task of the publication, without a doubt, must be to struggle for the eradication of harmful prejudices against women that are flourishing in our society and to coordinate efforts for the development and propagation of a different view of women—one that is healthy and corresponds to a greater degree to reality.

Some steps have been taken in this direction in the *Almanac Woman and Russia,* although for the moment they are still halting. The editors will pay more attention to this type of work in the future.

There is another important issue that the feminist publication is called upon to study (and the *Almanac* has successfully undertaken to do so) and that is the broad portrayal of the true position of our women—women of varying ages, social groups, and cultural levels. We also need a frank dialogue on the concrete problems that concern women, a dialogue free of hypocrisy and demagoguery. Inasmuch as the picture that the official press paints of our lives is badly distorted and every individual's experience is limited (particularly in our country, where the population's social and physical mobility is not great), every woman among us inevitably perceives certain sides of Soviet life in an absolutely false way, sometimes in the most fantastic ways. Experience indicates that we seldom have accurate perceptions about the existence or scale of other aspects of problems that every woman among us confronts. Often run ragged by the monotonous everyday hustle and bustle, we do not stop to think about this.

Vera Golubeva's essay makes a strong statement about this point. I have the sense that everything the author described I am also familiar with, but she has depicted certain experiences on a larger scale. This prompts one to do some serious thinking about one's own life and problems.

The range of questions touched on to one degree or another in the *Almanac Woman and Russia* is extremely wide. Naturally one cannot expect all the problems mentioned to receive sufficient attention. Some of them are merely listed, while others, in my view, are presented in a one-sided manner, in a very specific context.

I would like now to talk about the questions that have already been discussed in some way in the *Almanac* and to name some of the extremely widespread and pressing questions that, for the time being, remain outside the sphere of the *Almanac* and are awaiting resolution:

1. The extremely low level of sexual education and the lack of respect for and brutal attitude toward women in intimate relations that have become almost a norm for us,

2. The strange attitude toward sex that has taken root in our country: Officially, an almost puritanical purity is advocated, but in practice various forms of sexual activity flourish, which, because of the lack of education, constitute filthy depravity more often than not,

3. The terrible situation with respect to methods of birth control, which results in women being forced often to seek abortions,

4. The predominance of ostentation, by which everything is evaluated in a purely superficial way. Ostentation has a destructive influence on our personal family life in particular, since a great deal of effort is expended on maintaining "form." Many of our people are deprived of even the slightest glimmer of understanding of the true essence of life, which a person realizes in marriage, in the rearing of children, in romantic relations,

5. The epidemic passion for things and the greed that has overwhelmed our society lately (and this has occurred despite our low standard of living compared to that of other industrial countries),

6. The problems of various categories of women, arising from increasing corruption and speculation,

7. The problems that make men in our society passive and weak and what women can do to help men become more responsible in a way that will provide women with support and backing.

This list could easily be extended. There is, however, one problem of paramount importance, a problem that makes a feminist publication in our country at this time necessary and timely. In recent years an active and massive attack has been waged against women's current position in the work world. It has long been taken for granted that a woman will receive less money than a man for the same work. It is common to see a woman occupying a lower position than her male counterpart even though she is doing identical work. Women are only reluctantly hired for positions of responsibility. In recent years women have not been promoted to leadership positions on any level. On the contrary, they are being removed from these positions. As far as I can judge from observations and personal experience, this situation is now the norm everywhere, the result of a directive.

This fact alone is an outrage. It needs to be talked about loudly. We need to unmask the vile hypocrisy of our society that on the one hand brags about total equality between men and women in our country and on the other hand deprives women in practice of even those crumbs of equality they enjoyed until quite recently.

Translated by Rebecca Park

The Everyday Gulag[1]

THE EDITORS
Leningrad, Russia
Paris, France

In 1979 *Woman and Russia* became the first *samizdat*[2] to speak out on the everyday problems of Soviet women, problems that have long awaited resolution and have been largely ignored by the official Soviet press. These problems have developed into an everyday gulag for our women. The *Almanac Woman and Russia* received an extremely warm response throughout the world, but the reaction of the Soviet authorities was the opposite. The coworkers of *Woman and Russia* were subjected to numerous acts of repression, from summons by the KGB to arrests. After our own expulsion from the Soviet Union, the only feminist library in the entire country was confiscated from our editorial staff. Typewriters and original manuscripts of the four volumes of *Woman and Russia* were removed. In doing this, the authorities hoped to deprive us of our only means of producing and distributing our *samizdat,* since making Xerox copies is forbidden. Xerox machines are mainly found at military enterprises and unauthorized people making copies can be accused of espionage. As far as printing presses go, present-day revolutionaries are in dire straits: Our partocracy learned the lessons of the Revolution and knows how to combat revolutionary tactics. Unlike other organizations in the Soviet Union, the KGB takes an individual ap-

1. Gulag is an acronym referring to the prison camp system of the Stalin era. In this context it has been generalized to mean "prison."
2. Unofficial published writing, printed and distributed by the authors outside Soviet publishing houses.

proach to a suspected person. Equipped with electronic devices and highly trained specialists, the KGB studies thoroughly
the character of the victim and the psychological atmosphere
within the victim's family before launching an attack. The
Communist Party of the U.S.S.R. has in no way been outdone
by the Inquisition. The external methods have changed but
the purpose is the same. Natalya Lazareva and Natalya Maltseva were arrested in 1980 for their work on the *Almanac* and
are now free, thanks to our efforts.[3] But their activities have
been paralyzed because of the unrelenting pressure of the
authorities.

One simple old woman by the name of Olga Vinogradova
who had spent twenty-five years working as a radio communi-
cations technician was helping us. For this she was subjected
to threats and a treacherous search of her home. Our diaries,
photographs, and correspondence were in her home. Early one
morning zealous KGB agents threw our things in a large bag,
along with books from the old woman's library. Several months
have passed and she still cannot get her books back. We want
especially to draw the reader's attention to the fates of Kari
Unksova and Galina Grigoryeva, two faithful coworkers on
Woman and Russia who were also subjected to confiscations
and forced to go into hiding even though each woman has
children.[4] Two other women, Galina and Valeriya, gave Galina
Grigoryeva an interview upon their release from prison. (Their
interview was published under these names in the *Almanac*.)
They had been thrown in prison at the ages of eighteen and
nineteen, respectively, for parasitism and for not having an
official, legal address. They could not find work before and
they cannot find suitable work now, and so they risk being

3. N. Lazareva was arrested a second time on March 13, 1982, and on June
28, 1982, was sentenced to four years in a labor camp and two years of
internal exile.
4. Galina Grigoryeva has four children, including young twins. Kari
Unksova had two children.

arrested again on the same grounds. The solicitous little guys at the KGB do not want to leave them unattended, but, as everyone knows, this attention is costly.

We have succeeded in staying in touch with our coworkers, but only through unofficial channels, since the Soviet postal authorities intercept any mail of a remotely serious nature. By not using ordinary mail service, we do not subject others to unnecessary danger. Nevertheless, our women have such an acute need to voice their difficulties that within a short period of time after we came to the West, they sent us enough manuscripts for a fifth volume of the *Almanac* and for the international bulletin of *Woman and Russia*. The latter publication is not, incidentally, limited to Soviet authors but also contains articles by women of the so-called socialist camp. The women of Poland and Czechoslovakia are especially active, but women of Bulgaria, Romania, and Hungary also contribute. In Canada we recorded a conversation with a Chinese woman who was a visiting scholar at a Canadian university. We want to emphasize that the platform of our *Almanac* is pluralistic. We work with women of all convictions. Just as we listened to the Chinese woman express dissatisfaction with certain elements of her country's system, we must in turn listen to our women in official circles. One woman who worked as a secretary in the regional committee of the Komsomol (the Young Communist League) described the following episode. The regional committee was scheduled to receive a delegation from one of Leningrad's grammar schools. A man with whom our heroine had long worked turned to her and said, "Some old bags are going to be here. Get some coffee on the table for them." Even this woman who had grown accustomed to the cynicism of our Party members became inwardly indignant. She explained, "He spoke to me as if I were a robot without any feelings. And his words carried the scorn of a grandee, scorn for both the delegation and for me as a woman." Yes, emancipation has been proclaimed in our country, but it has not been realized on any level. For that reason, one of our humble demands is for 50 percent representation of women in the Politburo. Women constitute half the population of the Soviet Union and we produce and raise future generations; for these reasons alone we are entitled to 50 percent of the seats. The authors of a theatrical performance entitled *Mother and Woman of Russia* that was staged in Copenhagen by a group of Danish women understood the concepts of our movement very well. Plans were made to present the play in Wroclaw in 1982, but the military putsch of December 1981 brought an end to these plans. We had to show our support of the feminist movement in Poland.

We must not forget that the center of totalitarianism is located in Russia and our women are deprived of the elementary right to make their pain known to the public. Our *Almanac* gave women this opportunity and it became clear immediately (from the letters, articles, and declarations of these women) that a fundamental reorganization of our families is imperative. Our families, which fully preserve patriarchal traditions, must become egalitarian: men must not feel themselves to be masters but rather equally responsible with women for domestic duties. As early as the 1920s a proposal was made to pay people for doing housework, whether they be male or female. It should be remarked that in Sweden such a law has recently been passed, and Swedish men do not consider it a disgrace to take a maternity leave. But in the Soviet Union, which has loudly proclaimed itself a socialist government, women get a fist in their faces or a drunkard for a husband or harassment by the KGB instead of the help they need.[5] The more women protest, the greater is the pressure on them to shut up. Whether they be participants in a union movement like our

5. Recent legislation, enacted in 1981, allows a maximum of fourteen days' paid leave for each period of a child's illness (subject to the attending physician's written authorization). Fathers as well as mothers are eligible for this leave. This law indicates a more direct approach to equalizing child care responsibilities, but its practical effect remains to be seen.

SMOT,[6] like Valeriya Novodvorskaya and Natalya Lesnichenko, whether they be members of a Helsinki watch group, like Tatyana Velikanova and Tatyana Osipova, whether they be women fighting for religious freedom, like Nadyezhda Brykova and Tatyana Shchipkova, or whether they be members of an unofficial workers' commission fighting the use of psychiatry for political purposes, like Irina Grivnina (the initiator of such a committee) and Natalya Saveleva (the victim of such improper use), or whether they be participants in a drive for national independence, like Raisa Rudenko and Olga Matusevich, the result is the same—repression. These acts of repression do not overlook women in the world of art. Natalya Zhilina, an artist who took part in exhibitions by nonconformists, now finds herself poverty-stricken. Our well-known ballerina Alla Osipenko received an extremely severe warning when she offered her spacious apartment for an exhibit by artists "not recognized by the official culture," such as Natalya Zhilina. The list of persecuted women is endless. Mention should also be made of Malva Landa, Lyudmila Listvina, Oksana Meshko, the poetess Irina Senik, and our friends from the Baltic republics such as Zhenya Navitskaite and Onu Vitkauskaite, as well as Elena Bonner and the Jewish activist Ida Nudel. But one article or one speech is not enough. Amnesty International has been collecting documents about these things for some time and is doing everything possible for the release of the persecuted. Tatyana Mamonova, as editor in chief of *Woman and Russia,* has personally received steady support from branches of Amnesty International in Canada, England, Scandinavia, Switzerland, and France. We are pleased that we can work together for the good of humankind.

Translated by Rebecca Park

6. An acronym for an unofficial union called the Free Interprofessional Association of Workers. Its leader, Lev Volokhonsky, was arrested and charged with "spreading fabrications about the Soviet Union." At this writing he is in a Leningrad jail.

Actions and Counteractions

THE EDITORS
Leningrad, Russia
Paris, France

Our course is like the course of a long-distance swimmer. It is the result of two forces: the efforts of feminism (read "humanism") and the changing currents. It is hard to adjust to a new value system immediately, but the psychology of the individual equals the psychology of the group right from the very start. The majority of men are very reluctant to give up their customary privileges. Not everyone is born an August Bebel. But it is a rare man these days who openly dares to call himself a sexist. Sexism is now equated with racism and people of good will or those who pretend to be progressive are watching the phenomenon of feminism. The backwardness of everyday Soviet life generates the ugliest forms of interrelationships, and a superficial coating of culture will not alleviate the situation. The Soviet phallocrat feels no inhibition about being one. He does not even know such a category exists. The *Domostroi*[1] does not seem like a tangled jungle to our hero; he finds his way around just fine. Yes, he lacks information, but we will enlighten him in time. For when a civilized person panders to that kind of ignorance, that is sad.

We had the pleasure of receiving a correspondent from France-Presse and were struck by the lack of independence in his judgments. We were put on alert by a joke he made at our first meeting: "Feminism is the opiate of women." His joke betrayed a trivial understanding of the creative character of

1. A sixteenth-century Russian treatise detailing the proper role of women and including a section on appropriate forms of wifebeating.

235

the women's movement. But we were not prepared at our next meeting for his active assault on feminism with the aim of distorting it and adapting it to forms of anti-Soviet snobbery that have firmly established themselves in the underground.

First he asked with irritation why in *Femmes et Russie*[2] and *Rossianka*[3] Lenin's name is so often mentioned. (This, according to him, is unacceptable for *samizdat*.)[4] Were we not slanting the publication in a particular political direction? We answered him that Lenin's name appears no more often than any other; but if Lenin's name cannot be mentioned in *samizdat* publications, then *Woman and Russia* makes no claim to being what he defines as *samizdat*. Furthermore, our political slant is feminism, which is neither Leninism nor anti-Leninism. We asked him not to dwell on names. If we mention such people as Eva Braun, Freud, Golda Meir or Mao in our texts, this means no more than an analysis of world events. In response to this he asked, "Then give me your definition of feminism. List its goals and tasks." This is the same request, made in the same aggressive tone, the KGB made of me. I replied, "All right, but before that we would like to hear your definition of good and evil and also to learn the goals and tasks of truth." He answered me with another question. "What don't you like about Maria?[5] Are you an enemy of the Church or what?" My reply to this was detailed and elaborate.

We want to make it possible for all women to express themselves, to express their thoughts on one subject or another. We intend in the future to continue publishing both religious and

2. The French translation of the first volume of *Woman and Russia*.
3. The second volume of *Woman and Russia*. A different title was used to mislead authorities in the U.S.S.R. as to the identity of its authors.
4. Unofficial published writing, printed and distributed by the authors outside Soviet publishing houses.
5. Maria is a group of feminists, including several of the editors of the first *Almanac*, emphasizing a Russian spiritual approach to feminism within the framework of the Russian Orthodox Church. They have chosen the Virgin Mary as their symbol.

antitotalitarian articles in addition to other things. The small group Maria seeks to be viewed as the Slavic variation of feminism. But many feminist positions are merely being proclaimed in Maria. The basic strategy of this group is to strengthen and broaden Orthodox political positions both in Russia and in émigré circles abroad. The members also count on the international arena. History shows us that this little group is doomed by the lack of an overall approach to world phenomena. By emphasizing Orthodoxy, Maria takes the teeth out of feminist objectives. Reactionary circles both inside and outside Russia are already beginning to use Orthodox-political feminism as an ideological battering ram in the fight for chauvinistic hegemony. Solzhenitsyn has a curious note that Stalin restored old Russian epaulets and the Russian Orthodox Church. Slavophilism is slowly and imperceptibly becoming a cult (with all its special historical and traditional attributes). It is coming out in the form of kitsch through the art of the "officially recognized dissident" Ilya Glazunov and through various theatrical productions. This is an obvious attempt on the part of the present-day Orthodox to make their policy more flexible and effective and less odious and repellent. Meanwhile, not only has their political activity stayed the same but certain precepts have become even firmer.

It would be wrong not to notice a definite evolution in the ideology of feminist dissidents. This restructuring is the result of the broad response from around the world to the first feminist publication in the Soviet Union. The question is, what does this evolution mean and in what direction are the new tendencies developing? The small group Maria has dismantled feminist ideas. Theirs is an adulterated feminism designed to elicit a favorable reaction. The attitude of this group is extremely libertarian inasmuch as it is dictated by pragmatic, utilitarian goals of adaptation. Like Procrustes, Maria is trying to fit new social developments to a standard bed. The use of feminist terminology in their new journal does not conceal the deep deformations of the so-called unofficial culture, which has not come up with any more alternatives for women than has the official culture.[6] Maria's ideological growth has followed a zigzag path. Their mechanical reshuffling of ideas is only a camouflage that borrows the name of feminism. Even the most reactionary concepts have profited in one way or another from actual events and developments. The value of a free feminist publication is precisely the opportunity it offers to eliminate obsolete or bankrupt ideas. The old rags dragged out from the trunks of Slavophilism as well as the church scholasticism in the journal Maria are inconsistent with the essence of feminism—feminism that fills the lungs of thousands of women in the West with its bracing fresh air. But the number of women is not the issue. Even when that journal represents a minority of the population, the feminist vanguard is capable of actively reeducating society, of making radical improvements in women's consciousness. And it can also affect the consciousness of those men who would never have supported feminism and would not have understood the goals of feminism until some future experience had convinced them of the rightness, the naturalness, and the inevitability of the women's liberation movement.

Do we believe in national feminism? We believe in international feminism and we recognize every country—our country, an Asian country, the United States—has its own specific character. We understand that sexists are the same everywhere, though their plumage may vary. Women in every corner of the

6. The *unofficial culture* is a broad term used to describe art, literature, politics, and thought not recognized or accepted officially in the Soviet Union. Unofficial culture is sometimes specifically anti-Soviet. Other times it may simply refer to something too modernistic or controversial to be sanctioned by the official organs of culture. It encompasses the dissident movement, the nonconformists, the underground, the avant-garde, and the counterculture.

earth are subjected to the same terrorist act (rape) whether the rapist be a Russian or a German, a Frenchman or an African. This is universal. The elimination of all moral (immoral) factors that sustain phallocracy is the only goal for women of the world. Any belittling or distorting of feminist ideas means the strengthening of sexist ideology. This ideology is embodied in a very basic peasant proverb that says, "A hen is not a bird and a woman is not a human being." Everyone has grown so accustomed to this idea that no one even makes the logical leap to the sequel, "In that case, a rooster is also not a bird; who then *is* a human being?"

Women have long been the objects of shameless demagoguery. And feminism is not simply the rejection of patriarchal traditions. Principally it provides a new solution to the problems that confront the human race. By uncovering the causes that have produced a false world view, feminism indicates the ways in which the psychological slavery of women can be conquered. These ways dictate the destruction of old ideas on which the psychological slavery of women is based. Like the abolition of religion in our country, at first the emancipation of women was understood in an extremely primitive way. People suddenly got the idea that anything goes. The restoration of religion by the unofficial culture is a form of protest against the existing order (disorder). It is the more admissible (partially legalized) form of protest against a repressive government. But the concept of a believer is no longer what it used to be; rather it is amorphous and is interpreted by the unofficial culture in a variety of ways. For many, the return of the neo-orthodox followers of Christ is nothing more than a game. Alas, the game makes no demands that the "new Christians" be ascetics or outcasts. They often ignore the most elementary laws of mercy, especially in relation to women. Drunkenness, divorce, adultery, and the foulest, most abusive language are simply the order of the day in their world. Love between a man and a woman, to say nothing of friendship, is frequently considered banal in the Soviet Union. But to hit a woman in the face for being "disobedient" is not banal in the least. To rape her in a studio where an artist paints pictures of the saints and where images of these saints hang from the walls is no great sin. In general many of the "new Christians" thought it only natural to "give in to sin." And so the moral potential of our society has not been strengthened by the efforts of the new believers. One archpriest notes that "an absence of trembling at one's feelings of depravity" is characteristic for the majority of modern believers.

The majority of believers have an anthropomorphic concept of God. Not only does He resemble a human being, but He is a man. The following opinions expressed by a neo-orthodox follower from Moscow are not exceptional. He asserts, "A man introduces a source of divinity into love. If he loves a woman, then she becomes more spiritual. So homosexuality between men, let's say, is not as blasphemous as is female homosexuality. Love between two women is a terrible sin, because she is deprived of that source of divinity. Their sexual relations are totally lacking in any spiritual quality; it's bestiality plain and simple!" "Objectivity" like this is the best proof that religion, like any other patriarchal code of ethics, is one-sided. Christianity made a god out of their code of ethics, and moreover, a male code of ethics made a male god. This does not prevent Christianity from becoming increasingly "feminine" both in essence (submissiveness and obedience in the patriarchal structure are elements specifically attributed to the female nature) and in composition (according to our statistics, women constitute 75 percent of Church membership). The constancy of women's belief and the sharp reduction in the number of male members in Russian Orthodox communities have helped transform the structure of the Church. Now in many places women fulfill the duties of sacristans and are predominant among

Church elders. Not infrequently one sees women in "the holy of holies" [7] of a church or on the altar, which were previously barred to women. Even the Orthodox law that a woman can not visit a church until forty days have elapsed after she has given birth (if the child is female, the time period is doubled) is not as strictly observed as it used to be.

A lonely, despairing woman turns to the Church, while a man who has failed prefers alcohol. Of course, sometimes the two are combined. Tests of the social consciousness indicate that the belief in a paradise beyond the grave is firmer among retired women, housewives, and invalids, that is, among people who do not await a paradise on earth.

With the exception of those described above, it is the educated woman who comes to religion. Here we have the transfer of divine substance to the world of spiritual guests. After all, whole layers of our soul are unexplored—even outer space has been studied in greater depth. The scientific intelligentsia has a modified concept of the supernatural that presupposes an eternal predisposition to self-development. In our country, besides Christianity, we have Islam, Buddhism, and Judaism— in other words, a wide field from which to choose a religious object. The artistic intelligentsia's god appears more often in the role of a traditional fetish, relieving the believer of intellectual tension. By assimilating the latest swings in social moods, religion strives to maintain and consolidate its influence. It is becoming more modern, and we feel this is a good thing, since, in addition to everything else, it allows women greater access to its spheres. When women enter the Church and enjoy the full rights of membership, then inevitably a transformation of the Church and the entire religious complex will take place. The new female pastors in the West are undoubtedly a positive phenomenon. We are simply opposed

7. The "holy of holies" is the sanctum.

to the possibility of feminism being displaced by the Orthodox religion in Russia. Certainly, points of agreement will be found. But feminism and religion are diametrically opposed on important issues—on abortion and lesbianism at the very least.

The abstractly humanistic vagueness of the neo-orthodox theory may seem attractive after the daily barrage of political propaganda at work, in school, on the radio and television. Ironically, this constant propaganda drives Soviets to political indifference. Some of us have experienced a religious pull. We have attended church, observed religious holidays, and even toyed with the romantic idea of going into a monastery for self-perfection. A Soviet's spiritual life is now no less idealistic than it is religious. The workers at one time demonstrated great energy believing that they were building a society for themselves and for all workers. But after following specious phrases like "simplicity in life," the workers found themselves forced to exist for decades on a low standard of living in the name of a murky development plan or "defense." Undoubtedly they cannot accept this situation indefinitely. Furthermore, Stalinism thoroughly compromised the reforms of the Revolution, annihilating the brightest and most creative personalities in Russia and frightening the rest of the people. (Stalinism, in essence, was counterrevolutionary.) The generation of the 1930s was poisoned by mistrust and turned to mysticism. In the past, the abolition of religion, like the illusory happiness of the people, was a requirement for actual happiness. But Stalinism not only did not produce actual happiness, it also did violence to the people. Hence the popularity of vodka and the return to religion as well as the sports craze.

One hopes we will not return to Stalinism, though the warning signals are there. These signals are Stalin's reappearance in war movies, the return of his portrait in the studios of certain artists (after all, there is a semi-ban on this and it makes for quite a display of courage), and the appearance of the same portraits on the windshields of cars (and not only Georgian cars). There is something spicy about this, the portrait of a despot, calculated for its shock value. Perhaps all of this is limited to individual attempts at self-approval (purely male) and to nostalgia. Stalin's antinational policy did not prove his strength in the least but rather his inner weakness. An imperfect system always strives to isolate itself, shutting out contact with other systems in order to preserve itself. We will permit ourselves the following analogy: "Christ's commandments" versus the bloody Crusaders and "Lenin's bidding" versus the Black Marias[8] of Stalinism. Black cassocks have been exchanged for red, but the pastors keep on promising people the same bright future. The idea of Christian socialism, partially expressed in Alexander Blok's poem *The Twelve*, completes the picture. There is a grain of truth in both Christianity and socialism, but the illusory happiness simply does not become real. In order for an idea to be realized in life, you must have a society of spiritually mature individuals. People who have not matured enough to acknowledge public personal responsibility for what goes on around them will never progress to a defined goal. Deprived of props and supports (imagined or real), such people fall back to their starting point and may regress even further. When people become totally disappointed with the ideal, they are driven to dissolution (moral and physical). But who will undertake the transformation of society? People need certain conditions for growth. Who will create those conditions? It is a vicious cycle. Our Civil War bled Russia dry (beginning with the people's just indignation over the realization that the Revolution had turned into an unstoppable, abnormal process).

Conditions more favorable to the transformation of society arose, not in Russia, but in Europe and the United States. They arose in countries that had observed the historical process in Russia and had drawn their own conclusions. In N. G. Chernyshevsky's words, "Poverty and degradation hinder the develop-

8. Vehicles, formerly painted black, used to take arrested persons to and from jail; a patrol wagon.

ment of a worthy human life. Concern for the masses' well-being is a true means of developing the higher rewards that a human being is capable of valuing." The masses' well-being is of little concern to those who are pursuing their careers in the Party. They require of people under them an immediate, real return, and even their best intentions produce a vulgar utilitarianism. The importunity and rectilinear quality of propaganda is repellent. An understanding approach to the individual is totally lacking. The cold, bureaucratic approach of local committee members, Party committee members, and housing committee members (all these committees amount to the same thing) merely causes alienation and not infrequently inspires fear. The evil is not personified. Leadership and authorities on both large and small scales act in conformity with the "Party line."

When the correspondent of France-Presse asked us why the *Almanac Woman and Russia* rushes to criticize the unofficial culture and even reports the activists' names, we thought of the "secret line of the second party." [9] The people mentioned are not fighters for human rights, though they count themselves among the dissidents. The best proof of this is their crude sexist speech. We are not giving away anything new about them. We are simply stating well-known facts.

Practical humanism finds its brightest expression in the women's liberation movement. Women give society its very life, and in them duty and personal interest coincide (the revolutionaries' dream). Living for others, women in motherhood are naturally living for themselves as well. In the process of creating their own happiness, they are not acting contrary to the interests of others.

Translated by Rebecca Park

9. The author is referring to the conservatism and frequently hostile attitudes of nonconformists, dissidents, and other male members of the unofficial culture toward feminism.

Women and Peace

Two world wars and a civil war have been fought on Russian territory in this century. World War II had an especially devastating impact, with the death of at least twenty million Soviet citizens (about one in ten), the destruction of countless villages, towns, and cities, the slaughter or confiscation of livestock, and the deportation of millions of Soviets as slave laborers.

The war decimated the male population, leaving census figures of twenty million more women than men as late as 1959. Antiwar feeling runs high, especially among the survivors of the Nazi carnage. In cities such as Leningrad, which withstood a three-year German blockade with heavy civilian losses (at least 900,000), every older resident has a tale of heroism and horror to tell.

As the articles in this section indicate, the Soviet government capitalizes on the memory of World War II, a time of unprecedented national unity, to build popular support for its peace initiatives and for the maintenance of a large and well-equipped military. Special women's peace organizations, such as the Committee of Soviet Women, are encouraged, but they hew closely to the official line. Unofficial peace organizations have been crushed by the KGB. Nevertheless, it would be a mistake to underestimate the depth of antiwar feeling, especially among Soviet women. The Soviet government may well have to confront its own gender gap on this issue.

"We Need Peace and We Need the World"

EKATERINA ALEXANDROVA
Leningrad, Russia

"We need peace and we need the world, as much as possible," is a popular Russian anecdote.[1] Well said! This phrase captures the true spirit of today's Soviet foreign policy and the secret thought behind official pronouncements on the theme of peace.

These pronouncements, as is well known, are calculated for two groups of consumers. On the one hand they are calculated for outside, international groups. And sad to say, there are people on whom such pronouncements still produce an impression, one that serves Moscow. The outsider may simply believe what she or he hears. After all, other people are doing the deliberating. Who can figure them out and know what is going on over there? Maybe democracy really is bad for the Russian people. Truly, no matter what happens inside the Soviet Union, the speeches about the need for peaceful coexistence between countries of different social structures, about the Soviet government's tireless fight for peace, about the peace-loving policy of the U.S.S.R., about the urgent need to strengthen peace and friendship among nations, look very decent. They look decent, that is, if you have not paid attention to what is behind them. What is behind them, as is widely known, is the militarized character of the Soviet economy and, more important, the ex-

---

1. The anecdote from which the author takes her title is a play on the words *peace* and *world,* which in Russian are one and the same: *mir.* This anecdote appears to be calling for peace, but its listeners hear the word *world*—"We need the world, as much as possible."

pansionist character of Soviet ideology and public policy. In addition, there is the specific character of the thoughts and the psychological attitude instilled by forces "from above" in the minds of the Soviet people, for the people's consciousness must be carefully worked on in order to ensure stability and an environment in which a totalitarian system of the Soviet variety can function successfully. This carefully shaped consciousness is also necessary if this system is to spread and strengthen its influence in the outside world. And it is precisely the official pronouncements on peace, calculated only for domestic consumption, that to a significant degree fulfill this task of shaping the consciousness of the Soviet people in such a way as to be advantageous to the regime.

In the Soviet Union people are constantly talking on the radio, on television, and at meetings about the struggle for peace. They write about it in newspapers, magazines, and books. Banners with peace slogans hang everywhere, in the streets, in movie theaters, and in various establishments: Peace to the World!, Long live the peace-loving foreign policy of the Communist Party of the Soviet Union!, Long live peace and friendship among nations and so on.

For the average Soviet, the assertion that there is a constant, real threat of war from outside the Soviet Union has become a platitude, a given. As a rule, people do not give any serious thought as to how true this assertion is. They do not question it, but rather look on it as an objective reality, a fact of life, a phenomenon of the same order as green leaves on a tree, or dark nights and light days. This way of thinking is the result of many years of relentless propaganda by the Soviet mass media.

The idea of a very real threat of World War III has taken hold in the Soviet consciousness. And there is a firm belief not only in the threat of war but also in the idea that this threat comes specifically from the outside world, that the outside world by its very structure is hostile to and aggressive toward the Soviet Union. The Soviet government, on the other hand, is basically peace loving, and only under pressure of the most dire necessity has it been forced to strengthen its defense capabilities. (The terminology reveals little. You rarely read or hear about "the strengthening of Soviet military might." Instead the media talk about "the strengthening defense capabilities.")

It is well known that, according to Marxist-Leninist teaching, the constant threat of war in the modern world arises from "the world of imperialism." Soviet propaganda makes use of this thesis all the time, and on the whole, people believe it. They look skeptically at developed, capitalist countries and expect from them all manner of dirty tricks. Not long ago they added the Chinese to the category of world imperialists. (To the Soviet ear, "world imperialism" is practically synonymous with "American imperialism.") Inhabitants of the Soviet Union also strongly mistrust other yellow and black peoples, if for no other reason than that Soviets have such a vague picture of how things really are in other parts of the world. Soviets believe that before you have time to turn around, these people will be pulling some stunt!

To the Soviet, there is danger everywhere. And what kind of danger? Nuclear explosions, death, and total destruction— something so incomprehensible, so terrifying, so awful, that even to imagine this horror is impossible. In the best possible scenario there would be poverty, homelessness, hunger, cold.

Besides, the overwhelming majority of people have only the dimmest notion of what would really happen if another global war were to break out. That is the terrifying part about it. You can conjure up all the nightmare scenarios you want, to the limits of your imagination, but if you do not have much of an imagination, that is even more terrifying—total ignorance, a black hole.

In any case, this means an end to life as we know it, a life that, for the majority of Soviets, is nothing but unrelieved boredom, dreariness, and monotony. But in the face of possible nuclear war, their lives seem sweet, "prosperous," and good. Prosperous is another catchword. Thus, the more often you remind the people of war, the more they begin to value what they have and the less fuss they will make.

And who is saving the Soviet people and all of humanity from war? Who tirelessly stands guard for peace? None other than our very own Soviet government, of course. So the system has a lot of shortcomings (as they say in the fatherland), so the country is going to rack and ruin, there is still something to be glad about: The Soviet government is fighting for peace!

From this point it is just one step to another idea: "Hey gang, let's not bitch about our Soviet government. The international situation is *so* difficult! Just so long as we don't have a war! Compared to that, everything else is just a trifle. We'll make ends meet somehow."

How cleverly are people tricked into swallowing all this! It is the system that has reduced the Soviet people to their present deplorable state. But we should thank our very own Soviet government that we are still alive. No matter that we are living badly, we are still *living!*

Thus, the demagoguery that focuses on peace is an extremely effective method for maintaining some degree of the population's support and of securing a "moral-political unity between people and party." And all this is done under the extremely difficult conditions of failing internal policies and a bankrupt economy.

In its psychological attack on the people, the Soviet propaganda machine goes substantially further. It systematically and relentlessly instills Soviets with the idea that everything on earth exists thanks exclusively to the Party and the government. It is as if the Party and the government have usurped the role of the Creator, and if not the Creator, then whatever is the source of all living things. The sun shines, children run about, we sit at the table and eat our cabbage soup, and all this is due to the titanic efforts of the Party and the government. So thank you, Party; thank you, government. Thank you for everything—for the sun that shines above, for the little children born into the world, and thrice thank you for giving us something (for the moment) from which to make cabbage soup! While we are on the subject, another tool for propaganda, quite effective in the way it acts on people, is bread: "Bread is our benefactor," and so on. This concept is bound in the closest possible way to the subject of peace, so much so that in the minds of many Soviets the two subjects are inextricably intertwined. It is even articulated this way: "There's no peace so there's bread."

Let us reflect seriously on what a monstrous sham this is. After all, thanks to the fundamental characteristics of the Soviet system and to the inner springs that move Soviet society, the opportunity for an active, interesting life in the U.S.S.R. has narrowed sharply compared with what it used to be. Life has become flat and gray. Many forms of an active, interesting life have died off or are manifested only in an ugly, pathological form, for example, life in the criminal world. And people know this or sense it. That is exactly why some people drink. But in spite of the obvious grayness and boredom that reign today in Soviet society (the result of conscious policies), people almost forget about the deadening quality of life. In fact they practically rush, with tears in their eyes, to thank the Party and the government for those pitiful fragments of life they still have. The source of death is glorified as a source of life! It is a kind of gibberish. No, it is not gibberish but ordinary Soviet reality.

The idea that in a certain overall scheme, the world beyond Soviet borders is hostile to the Soviet Union is constantly instilled in the people. The average Soviet cannot imagine the outside world very well; association with it has been made extremely difficult and one-sided, and the Soviet feels this "peculiarity," this opposition to the outside world, acutely. On the other hand, it is also because of this that the Soviet feels a sense of community with other Soviets. After all, by force of circumstances he or she is in the same relationship to the outside world as they are. They have identical information about that outside world, too. The Soviet people are conflicted about a lot of things among themselves, as is well known. But in one respect they are united—in their objective opposition to the world beyond their borders. And they recognize this unity very clearly. Furthermore, for Soviet people, this forced, unnatural unity is easily capable of becoming a natural, reasonable, and even voluntary unity as soon as they can be convinced of a danger threatening them from without, of the outside world's basic hostility to them. With the help of this clever propaganda trick, the Soviet people feel united as troops guarding the fortress instead of feeling united as prisoners. Very simple and very effective!

The most essential, and perhaps the most difficult, task for the Soviet authorities is finding an effective platform capable of uniting the people. And it would seem that the opposition of the Soviet world to the world beyond is the only such platform. This sense of opposition was not dreamed up yesterday. It has been cultivated throughout the years of Soviet rule. But the tragedy is that it always works, and no less effectively now than it did thirty years ago. It works in spite of the positive vision that could have been used to justify this sense of opposition, for it could indeed have been justified by humanity's centuries-old aspiration to build a new society. This ideal has faded for Soviet people, to say the least. What remains are the undisguised hostility and aggressiveness, immutable feelings on which propaganda plays successfully and which are carefully cultivated in the Soviet people.

Needless to say, it is extremely advantageous to the Soviet authorities to foster in their people hostility toward the world. If they can transfer to international relations all the negative emotions that have developed in Soviet society from living a wretched life, then these emotions will not harm the system. For instance, the Soviet people's low standard of living can be partially blamed on the "intrigues of the imperialist world"; because of these intrigues, the country is forced to spend more money on defense. As a result, the authorities can direct the Soviet inhabitants' hatred toward remote, mythical enemies and away from the individuals truly responsible for the people's poverty.

The Soviet authorities also find it useful to promote the idea that there is danger to the Soviet Union in the outside world. By this they create a certain tension in the psyche of each individual and in the psychology of the Soviet people as a whole. And this tension allows Soviets' attention to be distracted from their circumstances of poverty inside the country as well as from their own personal "minor" difficulties and concerns, difficulties and concerns that are the direct result of the general state of affairs. This kind of tension is then lumped with a second kind of tension—the tension produced by the difficult, unnatural, stressful conditions of Soviet life. This first tension conceals and absorbs the second tension so that it escapes people's notice as a unique and separate thing. The Soviets' general feeling of tension from the circumstances of their daily life is shaped into a tension specifically caused by external danger.

From here the recipe is simple. The harder life gets, the more often it becomes necessary to remind people about external danger. As long as that is done, everything will work out fine.

The people's discontent will not turn actively against the system.

And it would appear that the authorities are acting precisely in accordance with this recipe. I really do not know how much international danger has increased in the past two to five years, but Soviet life has become substantially worse over that period and simultaneously the attacks by the Soviet propaganda machine have intensified appreciably and continue to intensify. This in turn serves to develop that same "tension from danger." People are constantly being reminded of war, of the possibility of one occurring and about its horrors. The burdens of the previous war are constantly being called to mind. Certain impressionable people, especially those who have the habit (harmful under Soviet conditions) of turning on the TV, tend to develop a neurotic fear of war.

The strongest, most concrete "frontal" attack in this scheme seems now to be directed at children, carried out during the course of their early education in government institutions. Several of my acquaintances have related (absolutely independently of one another) stories of how their little son or daughter would come home from school from time to time in tears, shaking from sobbing and exclaiming, "Mama, I don't want there to be a war!" The parents, of course, are horrified, since they are concerned about their child's emotional health but have no idea how to protect their child from psychological trauma.

A mind overwhelmed by neuroses, oppressed by constant fear—the mind of a forever nervous person—is incapable of viewing things soberly and is easily manipulated by those who speak to the tension and fear in the heart. One gets the impression that Soviet propaganda is taking advantage of this phenomenon to the utmost. To illustrate how propaganda might achieve these results, I will cite an example on a current topic. While riding in a tram I happened to hear a conversation between two half-drunk workers. They were talking about Poland and were both extremely malevolently disposed to what was happening in that country. Their rather incoherent remarks boiled down to the following three sentiments:

1. The imperialists want to unleash another world war and to seize power over the world.
2. The Poles are letting themselves be led around by the nose by world capitalism. Those bastards!
3. Therefore, justice itself demands that those Poles be taught a good lesson.

And so reason the representatives of the working class! And to top it all off, they were obviously unhappy with the system: The second half of their conversation focused on their personal dissatisfactions. In essence, they complained, "Here we've been saving up all our lives and don't have a fucking thing to show for it, but the bosses, they're living well." As the saying goes, no comment.

In this example another phenomenon is apparent, one that is organically inherent in the psychology of a person (and an entire people) shaped in this spirit. From the belief that the outside world is hostile and potentially aggressive it is only one little step to the point where the Soviet individual feels active hostility and aggressiveness toward the outside world. This little step is so tiny and so natural that it could escape notice entirely.

Hypnotized by the myth of external aggression, the person becomes dangerous and the source of active aggression. And if a person carries within a great deal of tension, it is natural for one to redirect this tension outward in order to relieve the inner tension and relax. What the Soviet draws in from the environment is passed on to another individual.

As a result Soviet society is storing up a huge potential for aggression, a potential that, objectively speaking, represents an extraordinary threat to humanity. But the tragedy of such an indoctrinated people lies in the fact that in their subjective view of the world, they do not recognize their indoctrination at all. In their subjective view, their nation is the defender of the highest, most humane values in existence. Objectively the aggressor cannot wait to go into battle. Subjectively, the noble knight sees a monster threatening humanity before him and a fight with this monster is a sacred duty. And the more terrifying this mythic monster is made to appear, the more real the danger seems to the deceived people.

The rhetoric of peace is linked in the very closest way with what in the U.S.S.R. is called the military-patriotic education of the people. And strangely enough, these two concepts combine splendidly. The military-patriotic education of the people is nothing more than the education of people in an openly militaristic spirit. With respect to American and Chinese dangers (as well as others), the military propaganda, whatever its specific content, not only does not shock anyone but is even accepted as something perfectly natural and moral to the highest degree.

The history of the Soviet Union has shown us that apparently the only positive feeling the system is capable of giving a person is the positive emotion of "walking in the common ranks." This should be understood in both the literal and figurative sense of the phrase. People see themselves as participants in a great common cause, and so on. The "love of marching music" and "love of ranks" (Solzhenitsyn's words, which capture beautifully the essence of this phenomenon) have been quite effective in unifying Soviets for years. If you observe today's Soviet propaganda, you get the distinct impression that "the people on the top" have once again taken to instilling these "virtues" in people in the most active way. The "love of marching music" and "love of ranks" form the hobbyhorse on which today's powers ride in order to give the people something positive, to draw them away from their ideological and psychological crisis, and to preserve the positions of those in power. And as sad as this may be, experience shows that from the lack of anything else positive in Soviet life and from its stupefying boredom, many people, especially older boys, are quite enthusiastically prepared to walk in the ranks, in the most literal sense of that phrase.

The military romance of live action and the alluring possibility of adventure as well as the special sense of unity among people marching together are just about the only positive things that remain for Soviet youth. This is evident even in the works of official art. (An impressive example of this is the film by Mikhalkov-Konchalovsky, *Slave of Love,* which won several awards at film festivals and created quite a stir.)

Lately the "military-patriotic education" has been sharply expanded and has taken on absolutely obscene forms and dimensions. Over here we sometimes listen to Soviet radio, only to be unpleasantly surprised. They are constantly praising military service and talking about military valor, patriotism, and so on, especially in broadcasts about young people. And recently we heard a new Soviet song that states directly, "Real men look good in a military uniform." Boom . . .

Thus, under the cover of the rhetoric of peace, not only is the military-industrial potential of the Soviet Union growing, not only are communities abroad being deceived, but the Soviet people are being made absolute fools of and the military policy of the Soviet Union is methodically turning the people unwittingly into a weapon through a relentless program of education.

Translated by Rebecca Park

The Peace March: East and West

TATYANA MAMONOVA
Paris, France

I have just returned from Scandinavia, where I learned that the Soviet government has agreed to the peace march from Oslo to Moscow. Many look on this venture skeptically, claiming that nothing will come of it and that the Soviet people will be isolated from the two hundred demonstrators with their incomprehensible signs in foreign languages. Perhaps the march for peace will not have the same repercussions as did the march Scandinavian women organized last year from Copenhagen to Paris. I participated in that demonstration and it had quite an impact even though all of Paris is generally on vacation in August. Whole families walked along together, tired but happy in their unity. And later, a wave of thousands of people demonstrating for peace swept over Europe. The Netherlands raised the entire population to its feet. The émigré paper *Russkaya Mysl'* [1] expressed anger that German pacifists gave American generals an unfriendly reception. And meanwhile banners in Bonn demanded that *both* the United States and the Soviet Union disarm.

Peoples of the world are feeling the need for détente especially acutely now. Paralleling the efforts of Scandinavian women, Italian women in Rome were submitting a proposal for a march for peace from West to East. Yes, undoubtedly the pessimists are partially correct in saying that this demonstration will be like the Olympic games in Moscow, when the or-

---

1. A weekly newspaper published by émigrés in Paris.

261

gans of control were giving all Soviet citizens intensive political training on how to conduct themselves with foreigners. No, this peace march to the Soviet Union may not have as many participants as one would like. But we must start somewhere. Can we sit around with arms folded and watch humanity slide off a cliff? Personally I am heartened by the Western women's initiative, and there are people in the U.S.S.R. who are capable of understanding this act correctly.

In the fall of 1982 the Paris publishing house Denoel released the fourth volume of the *Almanac Woman and Russia*. This volume contains a letter by Soviet feminists addressed to the official representative of the Committee of Soviet Women at the 1981 congress in Prague. I would like to cite a passage from that letter: "We have heard all our lives that our government takes care of its women and children and about how it works to see that women are healthy and that children grow up happy, without knowing the horrors of war, hunger, and injustice. But in the children's encyclopedia entitled *What Is This? Who Is That?* it says on page 42 of the first volume, 'Every little boy must prepare himself to become a good soldier in our Soviet army.' In our kindergartens and primary schools hymns about World War II and the Soviet army and navy are sung. By fostering a feeling of aggression in the children now, they can later send them off to confrontations not only with the Germans but also with the Chinese, the Americans, the Poles, or the Afghans." For my part I wish to add that the majority of our people, to this day, do not realize what happened in Czechoslovakia in 1968. After all, that was when the period of liberalization in the Soviet Union came to an abrupt halt, when the hopes of people of the so-called socialist camp for a true socialism were destroyed, and when our dissidents banded together. What happened in Hungary in 1956 could not have elicited serious protests from the Soviet people, because they had not yet had time to come to their senses after the long gloom of Stalinism. But Czechoslovakia of 1968 engendered an intellectual ferment that is still being suppressed.

The idea of a free feminist publication in Leningrad came about during that period as a reflection of general unrest and new self-confidence. It is noteworthy that it is revolutions that enable women to reach their full stature and to speak with a clear voice. Whether we take the French or the German or the Russian Revolution, in every one we discover masses of women coming to life and the brightest female personalities. These revolutionary outbursts in the historical process exacerbate certain hidden phenomena in social life—hidden dissatisfaction. The year 1968 is remembered not only for what happened in Czechoslovakia but also for the student strikes in Paris and feminist demonstrations in many countries around the world. International feminism has by no means hit a slump, as some people claim. The spontaneous feminist movement has found concrete applications. Throughout the countries of Western Europe and in America, special offices have been opened where women can receive legal advice, shelter, escape from a spouse's tyranny, and emergency medical treatment.

In fighting pornography and in defending the right to choose one's own method of birth control, the right to abortion, and the right to lesbian and gay relationships, feminism widens its scope to include other current problems such as ecology, alternative youth movements, and militarization. The military Putsch in Poland shows us that the militarization of society in any country is dangerous regardless of whether the country calls itself communist or anticommunist. Is there any difference between Pinochet and Jaruszelski? People suffer under the arbitrary rule of generals, whether they be Chileans or Poles. Expansion by the Soviet Union or the United States has the same consequences for lesser nations whether they be Afghanistan or Vietnam. The intensifying of the arms race instills fear in all people who are concerned with the future of humanity.

It is imperative that we search for paths of mutual understanding instead of rattling sabers. Countries must not seek to act from a position of strength, for this can lead to a tragedy ten times the magnitude of World War II. By virtue of her nature, woman is the preserver of life and thus it is logical that she should work actively for the defense of peace. The peaceful demonstration held by American feminists in front of the Pentagon is unforgettable. No less impressive was the antiwar demonstration in the summer of 1982 in New York City. Some 800,000 people participated.

Our sense of responsibility for our children compels us to take to the streets with our demands for peace. Consider the obvious motive: What are they filling our TV screens with? Whether it is the socialist camp or the capitalist camp, they are filling our screens with violence. In various permutations, some with moral themes, others without, our TV screens are bursting with shots and explosions, earthbound and cosmic battles. Our children learn about the world through a cruelty that is trivialized. The patriarchal society trains them to value the regalia of generals and supermen who seem to know nothing of spiritual values but only of the merit of the fist. From their earliest years children grow used to the game of death. Human beings lose all moral criteria, and are lost in the bottomless pool of cheap movies and TV serials. Adventure and diversion—that is what the pistol has become in the hands of the patriarchy. Next to this idol, the human diminishes in size and then turns into dust before the neutron bomb or the hydrogen bomb or the atomic bomb. The cynicism of arms sales poisons the atmosphere of our planet. The madness of the fanatics of evil sows skepticism among ordinary people. Young people have already given up believing in the future. We feminists do not wish to bow to fatalism because we know that much depends on us and because we know that a person always faces a dilemma: whether to build or to destroy. To destroy is simple and fun, but afterward there is nothing left. To build is not always easy and not always fun, but afterward something has been created, something that pleases the eye or helps to sustain life. Given the choice of love or hate, we naively choose love. We choose love that is ridiculed, cursed, and trampled upon but that always returns from ashes to become again as splendid as when it began. We have freed ourselves from religion, and now we want to love, not a threatening symbol, but each other. We refuse to forsake life on earth for a paradise beyond the grave. Our *Almanac Woman and Russia,* the first publication in the Soviet Union to give women the right to finally speak their minds, is dedicated to these secret aspirations. The authorities could not make up their minds to call the material in our *Almanac* fabrications, although that is exactly the way they define *samizdat* publications. Instead they called it tendentious and ideological. By that they apparently were referring to our tendency toward unity and solidarity and our ideology of peace and justice. Our modest words of truth in the *Almanac* made a strong impression on people, and did so without any recourse to loud slogans. And those words continue to ring out despite all the efforts of the authorities to stifle them.

The simple words of truth helped us to find friends in every corner of the earth. We hail France, which has chosen the path of socialism, and we hope that French socialism will be more open, more sincere, and more genuine than socialism in the Soviet Union. Personally I find the feminist Huguette Bouchardeau to be the most sympathetic figure in today's France. She proposes a program of ecological reforms as well as antimilitarism. We hail Greece, which has finally gained victory over the dark forces and has proclaimed freedom on the lips of Melina Mercouri, the remarkable actress and minister of culture. These women embody our future. We also hail Spain.

In the troubled 1980s, when the threat of war is constantly flaring up—whether it be in the Middle East, Latin America, Ireland, or Poland—it is especially important to cultivate the idea of peace in the hearts and minds of our children.

Translated by Rebecca Park

CONTRIBUTOR'S BIOGRAPHIES

CONTRIBUTORS' BIOGRAPHIES

GALINA GRIGORYEVA [1] is a psychologist by training. The mother of four children, she is raising them alone. Galina has been a participant in the feminist movement since the appearance of the first volume of the *Almanac* in 1979. The KGB has questioned her and searched her home, confiscating manuscripts and her typewriter. She is currently studying religion, yoga in particular.

LUDMILA KUZNETSOVA's life is striking and special, but her background is unusually typical, as if proving the teaching that anyone with the will, life force, and desire for freedom can do anything. Out of curiosity, Goricheva once did an informal sociological study and found that the majority of left artists, poets, composers, and political dissidents came from military and KGB families. Nowadays, sin and retribution follow more quickly.

Ludmila was born into the family of the head of the special section of the Cheliabinsk KGB. That is, her papa controlled and punished the punishers themselves—the executioner, as it were, raised to the second power. And Cheliabinsk is a major Urals industrial center, so his harvest was plentiful.

Ludmila graduated school with a gold medal for excellence, despite the most trying conditions at home. It was the end of the Stalin era, and her traumatized father could not cope with his significant reduction in rank. In the evenings, having rested and preparing for night duty, he organized a little domestic rehearsal, a three-hour interrogation of his unloved daughter, forced to stand before him and monotonously answer why she received a four,[2] why yesterday ... and so on. As a result, she lost her ability to speak and contracted tuberculosis.

Somehow healing herself, Ludmila left for Moscow, where she had been accepted into one of the toughest and most prestigious higher educational institutions, The Bauman Technical Institute. We'll skip over that period during which the young engineer Ludmila Kuznetsova tried to find her niche in official life and discover her personal destiny. Her real calling became apparent in 1974 when she fell in with a group more of friends than like-minded people, united by a general countercultural pathos, moral unity, and high creative potential.

Kuznetsova organized a salon, soon became the center of Moscow cultural life and began to write her own little essays and stories. Carefully studying classical and contemporary literature and fine arts, she had the courage to avoid participation in the "concrete struggle" for the right

1. Biographical material and photos for all the contributors are not available. The continued harassment by the KGB of feminist activists in the Soviet Union has made secrecy and the use of pseudonyms necessary.
2. In the Russian school system, students are graded on a scale from one to five with five the highest mark.

of self-determination with the intellectual elite of both capitals—Moscow and Peter (Leningrad). In her creative work and her public activity there always remains a natural quality: the knowledge of a friendly and caring person, ardently loving art but never hiding from anyone her provincialism or her position as an artistic "neophyte." And for her creative work, Kuznetsova intends to "lower herself" by associating her name with the ironic type of simple woman from a vulgar bourgeois background, endlessly touching in her untogetherness and social failure, her attempts to make it in this life pitilessly torn to shreds in the spokes of the state machine, or by the stupidity and feeblemindedness of the conformist milieu.

Thus are born these small masterpieces, short stories, like tales, a bit reminiscent of the work of Zoshchenko and Harms, different in their femininity, warmth, and humanity but similar in their tough and merciless self-irony and self-analysis. Aesthetes might be turned off by such simple, uncomplicated texts, but a genuine connoisseur, we are sure, could never miss their inner substance, the "feeling for the typical," and their original humor. Several of her *"mots"* of the type, "no money, my kidneys hurt," have already become proverbial in Moscow circles.

Intensive contacts with artists in Moscow and Peter, the endless search for a few pennies to live on, raising her daughter, the creation of a salon, the incessant scandals of communal apartment life, persecution and badgering on the part of the authorities and the K . house arrests, organizing the exhibit and festivals "Moscow-Paris," the first international endeavor uniting Russian art with the rest of the world, readings and long creative discussions, constant studying, press conferences, struggles with state organizations for the right to educate her child, and finally fifteen days in solitary and a hunger strike—this is the "creative atmosphere" in which these short stories and five chapters of the important novel, *Zinochka*, were written.

The manuscript for *Zinochka* was lost in a fire, started in her room by a neighbor, a KGB plant with no qualms about taking someone else's raincoat from its hook in the communal hallway or stealing for the night someone else's television from the closet near the kitchen. The KGB picked up Ludmila's eleven-year-old daughter in a store and questioned her for four hours. Ludmila's automobile tires were slashed. Her hands were broken in order to get some documents compromising the KGB and the police hidden in her bra.

As in the past, Ludmila works and writes around the clock. She collapses sometimes, her senses dulled, and lies with the telephone on her stomach while continuing to work. From a frightened little creature, timidly parrying the first attacks at her first interrogation, she has been transformed into a fighter of rare fearlessness and personal courage.

In her own perhaps comic way, she fights piggishness everywhere, even in prison. While in solitary confinement, she scraped obscene inscriptions from the walls and windowsills of her cell.

"Zinochka Expands Her Circle of Bohemian Friends" is the only fiction in *Women and Russia.*

Written by Kari Unksova
Translated by Sarah Matilsky

TATYANA MAMONOVA. I was born on December 10, 1943, in the village of Likhoobrazovo, in Yaroslavl province, in "evacuation." The feeling of a free childhood among the chickens, green berries, and a fierce bull, whose nose I wiped with my handkerchief (so say my parents), remains. But the war was also felt there. They say that once I ran in and, not yet able to speak, started to wail, "Sorrow, sorrow, trouble, trouble." Apparently, in the house next to ours a woman had received a condolence letter and her suffering made a strong impression on me.

My mother was a bookkeeper. My father was a lawyer. Neither could adjust to life. My mother, a graceful and by nature lively woman, was constantly worn down by the difficulties of life. The postwar Stalin years, with their poverty and untruths, did not affect our family in the best way. Father somehow "broke down" and, not having sufficiently satisfied his ambition, escaped into drunkenness. My brother, three years younger than I and by nature weaker, began early to lean toward hypocrisy.

I did not like school. I remember it as something dark and burdensome. But feeling sorry for my mother, I got by, though without interest. In my last years of school this unnatural, tense existence led me to develop a neurosis with the symptoms of erythrophobia, which left me absolutely unable to communicate. But by sheer strength of will I passed my final exams. My mind awakened only after I graduated from school. Still, out of sheer inertia, I enrolled in a pharmaceutical institute (I was to some extent interested in medicinal herbs), in the evening division, and got a job as a lab technician in the same institute, in the Department of Antibiotics. But my real interests lay in completely different areas. I wrote poems and drew. I became interested in linguistics (here my attempts to follow through on this quickly came to nothing: I was not accepted at the Leningrad University language lab—the only place at that time with language tapes—and they refused to let me visit my Polish friends, with whom I intended to practice conversational Polish).

My inner liberation led me to a passion for sociology. Although here, too, I encountered obstacles but I also learned what was the root of all evil. Outwardly still immature and not self-sufficient in practical terms, I acquired an independent spirit. My work in Leningrad television, my involvement in the Knowledge Society on Liteinyi Prospekt, my publications in *Komsomolskaya Pravda* and my wide-ranging correspondence (including the editor in chief of the journal *Zhenshchiny Mira* [Women of the World], to whom I revealed my longstanding feminist tendencies) did not yield practical results. I began to travel a lot, hoping through the kaleidoscope of impressions to find myself. But I found no kaleidoscope. Instead, in the Carpathians, in Central Asia, and on Kamchatka, I saw gray masses, over whom fluttered one and the same slogan; I observed epidemic drunkenness and heard everywhere the most vile curses insulting the virtue of women. The beauty of nature could not dim this panorama. All this was aggravated even further by the fact that as a single woman traveler, conditions were suicidal. It was impossible to stay in any hotel in the entire country.

Once more I settled in Leningrad and applied to work in the poetry department of the journal for youth, *Aurora*. Everyone figured that they would eagerly take me: I, without any higher education, landed a cushy job! But just as I had left the pharmaceutical institute because they studied the history of the Communist Party more than medicinal herbs, so I left *Aurora* because, despite their promises, they would not risk printing my poems. Besides, the editing and translating I had to do were not satisfying; the more so because even in this sinecure it was necessary to elbow your way to the top, which always sickened me. True, I must note that there were some bright moments: At the Seminar of Young Writers my verses were ardently supported by V. Betaka (a member of the jury), my translations of Prévert were welcomed by Tatyana Gnedich, and Efim Etkind invited me to participate in a poetry reading. I might name others as well, but I fear for their safety.

After leaving *Aurora*, I joined the movement of nonconformist artists and with them had my first exhibition. I was full of enthusiasm and inspiration, expecting to find among these people nobility and an uncompromising spirit. But several caused me to have doubts. Igor Sinyavin and A. Ivanov decided to snub me because of "women's inferiority." I encountered similarly blatant sexist tendencies among the avant-garde poets (V. Nesterovsky is the foremost representative). After these experiences, I was convinced of the importance of feminism; later my conviction grew through my access (thanks to the diplomats) to the Western press, which proved to me the significance and seriousr ss of the women's democratic movement. I came logically to the publication of the *Almanac Woman and Russia,* having lost faith in the official press and finding no support among members of the unofficial art movement, where my name was indiscriminately linked with that of K. Lil'bok, the sadist and rapist who now calls himself a dissident. I realized that our women, living in isolation, could not summon enough energy to continue to publish the *Almanac* and resolved to begin its publication in the West, uniting it with international feminism.

Translated by Sarah Matilsky

ALLA SARIBAN was born in Odessa in 1948.

In 1972 she graduated from Leningrad State University with a degree in biophysics, and in 1978 she received her doctorate in chemistry from Moscow State University.

Active in the feminist movement since 1980, Ms. Sariban has written several perceptive analyses of the position of women in the Soviet Union.

TSOVINAR TSOVINYAN (her friends call her Tsovik) is twenty-six years old.

She writes poetry in Armenian and, in addition to her native language, knows twelve languages.

Ms. Tsovinyan is not married.

KARI UNKSOVA is a talented writer of poetry and prose. Her writings have gone into the third and fourth volumes of the *Almanac Woman and Russia*. Kari has been known in artistic circles in Leningrad, Moscow, and the Baltic since the unofficial art movement began. The most piquant experiments in modern culture found vivid expression in her special, creative work. She was also interested in pop music (she told me about the most unique jazz ensembles), avant-garde poetry, and the painting of nonformists.

Kari Unksova, threatened with arrest, was forced to go into hiding. She is the mother of two children, a teen-age daughter and a very young son. She and her husband have an egalitarian relationship; he is sympathetic to her need for inner freedom. The authorities made several attempts to frighten Kari. On November 22, 1980, they sentenced her to fifteen days[3] in Leningrad. Four zealots from the KGB crudely staged "the hooliganism of Kari Unksova" at her address. She accused the four militiamen of assault and battery. The judge refused to hear the case. It was reviewed in another court of law, but Kari Unksova had to serve fifteen days. Later her apartment was searched and a typewriter, notebooks, letters, manuscripts, and books were removed. At that particular moment Kari was out of town and by force of circumstances was unable to return to her family.

In order to present Kari's activities more accurately I wish to cite the words of a very close friend, Svetlana Darsalia: "Kari Unksova is a poet who occupies a very distinct position in this world. Her poetry is distinguished by a deep philosophical subcontext. She is a person who stands outside of time, leaving it behind, and outside of space, recognizing no limitations of form. A true artist, she wants an open forum. Her words bear the pain of a prophet and a warning to a withering sensitivity and a consciousness that is falling asleep. All of Kari's creative work bears a messianic character. It's terrifying to think that humanity could make yet another irreparable error for which it will also have to pay."

The editor wishes to draw the readers' attention to the fate of Kari Unksova and prevail upon them to raise their voices in defense of other persecuted fighters for elementary civil rights.[4]

Written by Tatyana Mamonova
Translated by Rebecca Park

3. A sentence of fifteen days is imposed for lesser offenses such as drunkenness, fighting in the streets, or vandalism. This is a forced labor program whereby convicts are taken out of confinement for the day in order to perform work for the state, such as cleaning streets or working on construction sites.

4. Offered an exit visa in August 1982, Kari Unksova was informed by the authorities that she, her husband, and children, aged eight and seventeen, could leave by July 19, 1983. On June 3, Ms. Unksova was hit and killed by a car in Leningrad.